WHAT WOULD THE WORLD BE WITHOUT WOMEN?
STORIES FROM THE NINTH WARD

by Waukesha Jackson

Neighborhood Story Project
New Orleans, Louisiana

Other books from the Neighborhood Story Project

Before and After North Dorgenois by Ebony Bolding
Between Piety and Desire by Arlet and Sam Wylie
The Combination by Ashley Nelson
Palmyra Street by Jana Dennis

Series Editor: Rachel Breunlin
Graphic Designer: Gareth Breunlin

What Would the World Be Without Women
ISBN 1-933368-32-2
ISBN-13 978-1933-36832-0

Let us hear from you. www.neighborhoodstoryproject.org
Neighborhood Story Project
P.O. Box 19742
New Orleans, LA 70179

Soft Skull Press, Inc.
55 Washington St, Suite 804
Brooklyn NY 11201
www.softskull.com

Distributed by Publishers Group West
www.pgw.com

Text pages produced on 70 lb. Lynx Opaque, Smooth Finish,
donated by Weyerhaeuser Company, Fort Mill, South Carolina
Tango Coated Cover, donated by MeadWestvaco, Stamford,
Connecticut, manufactured in Covington, Virginia
Printing and binding donated by WORZALLA, Stevens Point,
Wisconsin USA

DEDICATION

THIS BOOK IS FOR EVERYONE WHO IS STRUGGLING, ESPECIALLY
MY MOM. KEEP YOUR HEAD UP, AND TELL YOUR STORIES.

ACKNOWLEDGEMENTS

I want to thank God first for keeping me here and guiding me in class everyday.

My Grandma and Grandpa, for staying on my back and taking me into your home and caring and providing for me. I'm very grateful even though sometimes I don't show it.

Thanks to my mama for wanting to get your life together. All of your actions made me so strong. Thank you for talking so honestly for my book.

Thanks to my Grandpa Frenchie for taking care of me when I didn't have anyone else to go to.

Thanks to Melva, for reminding me of my mother in so many ways.

I want to thank Reyond, Ceyond, and Teyond for being so sweet.

I want to thank my brother Mike for keeping me on his side and my brother Rodney for holding me down.

I want to thank Jamal Davis for inspiring me through good times and bad.

Thanks to Gwana Green for keeping me close and pushing me to be the best dancer I can be.

Thanks to Ms. Wells for all of the talks.

Thanks to the school and faculty of John McDonogh, for always running me to class.

Thanks to my friends—you're the best.

Thanks to Arlet, Ashley, Ebony, Jana, and Sam: I love you all and I'm so proud that we all finished.

And thanks to the Neighborhood Story Project, for the experience of writing a book about my life, and for teaching me how to cope with a lot of my struggles. I'd like to thank Abram and Rachel for interview edits, photography and help editing my book. And to Rachel, especially, for stressing me to write and for recognizing everything that I tried to hide, and letting me know that it was okay to let it go.

TABLE OF CONTENTS

INTRODUCTION

When I first decided to write this book I thought it was going to be easy and fast, like a class assignment. My goal was to just staying on one topic. I don't know where I got that crazy idea from, because that was not the eagle. Everything changed about what I thought was going to happen. Things got personal as I began meeting and exploring the world. In class, we talked, we laughed, we fought, we cried but we came a very, very long way from where we began.

The fear of talking about my life was hard to overcome. I didn't know what people would think about me afterwards. In the past, I've looked at the situation as though, "It could have been worse, and I'm still making it." I didn't want people to feel sorry for me or treat me differently because of my life experiences. I didn't want it to be like that because I am very strong and that response was just going to make me mad.

Before I started writing, I felt like there was just a big load on me. I was dealing with my mother and the different ways she abused herself, while living with my grandma who was disappointed in my mom and always worried about me.

Day by day as I worked on the book, there were questions asked about my mom. The more I avoided talking about her, the more I wanted to say. I got tired of all the questions, and I felt that I had to let it go. Talking and writing about things just made me feel better and made a better perspective for my life.

To me, mothers are the most important parent in a girl's life. While my daddy's barely been in my life, there have been times when my mother has taken care of me. When she wasn't there, I missed her in lots of small ways. I missed her telling me what to do, talking and laughing, and playing together. Not having her around to do things made me feel really lonely.

Thinking about my relationship with my mom made me reflect on how it's usually the woman's responsibility to take care of children, whether you have a father or not. You'd be surprised these days if a child's mother and father are still together. It's not a big deal if a family is without a father, but when people find out you are not staying with your mom, they'll have some sympathy and ask, "Are you all right" or "Do you get the proper care-taking you need?" While it's painful not to have your mom around, a lot of kids these days are staying with their grandparents because they are without both parents.

In this book, I'm going to look at my relationships with women in my family and how they cope with life and struggles. Women are always doing this and doing that and just taking care of everything. They deal with losses while juggling their other responsibilities at the same time. I want to learn how to do that, too. Women do things and most times don't get any credit, but what would life be without any women? I wanted to honor them in this book. I also talked to my neighbors and close friends about their struggles in life and how they got through them. I wanted to know how women took care of their families and their communities in my part of town. In the process, I learned how to deal with the loneliness that I feel about not having my mom, and I can begin to go on with my life.

PART I: WOMEN IN MY FAMILY

What you are about to read is typical life experience through good and hard times. Like my life, this story starts with my mother. We talk about all of the houses I've lived in and how I came to live on North Miro Street in the Ninth Ward with my grandmother.

My grandmother has her own set of stories, from growing up in the Seventh and Ninth Wards, to living in the Florida Projects to owning her own home. And she has stories about her four children. Two sons have died in her home after long periods of sickness. She has feared the worst for her older daughter—my mother—and is just beginning to have hope for her again.

We also talk to my Aunt Melva, and get her perspective on my grandmother and my mother. She knows how to get along with both of them, and I admire her for being able to be close to both of them.

I've felt distant from everybody because I've been alone, without my mother, for much of my life. It's been hard for me to be happy around other people for a long period of time. I interview my mother and talk with her about her life and my feelings of abandonment.

This is an explanation of my relationships with the women in my family, because they are the people that I have felt the most comfortable with. The women in my life are close, and have survived, and are here to tell their stories.

MY MOTHER

My entire life my mom has been on and off drugs, and I have been with and without a mother. There have been times when she has been there for me and times she wasn't. When she wasn't high, her entire life was like a natural rush. She liked to get into things and would go to fairs and Six Flags and ride all the roller coasters. I was always the scared one but I would get on the ride because my mother made me feel safe. She would always sit by me and hold my hand.

My mother is very straight up. She doesn't bite her tongue, and she doesn't let anyone run over her. Whenever I went out with her she stopped and talked just because she saw somebody she knew. She likes to laugh a lot and tells side jokes about you, like if your feet were big or something. She didn't finish high school, but it seems like she knows everything. When I've had reports to do for school, I went to her to ask something about it and she would have tons of things to say, and it would become my whole report.

Some of my favorite times with her have been sitting on the floor in her room while she sits on the bed doing my hair. She knows how to do all sorts of hairstyles like straw curls, pin-ups, and spirals. She fusses at me, "Put your head down!" and yanks it to the position she wants. Despite her handling my head, this is our closest time. She always asks what's going on in my life, and she checks in with me about how she's feeling too. We have our own rituals. She'll cook meat sauce and spaghetti when I'm not feeling well with cramps. We'll sit in the living room watching *Love and Basketball*. Every time we watched it she always huffed and puffed and smacked her teeth because she wanted to watch something new, but she still hung out with me on the couch.

I always wished that she would think of her kids and just drop her bad habit, but it never happened. You know how you watch TV shows, and they would usually have a family such as a mom, dad, and kids? I would think about my situation and cry sometimes. I wished for a real mom and dad, but they were rarely there. As a child growing up, you always need someone to help with homework. I only had Mike, but I needed my mom. I had to dress myself and learned to comb my own hair at four years old on a day when my mom wasn't there. With personal things I always did for myself, but for the grace of God my mother was around when I became a young lady at 12 years old. I learned to love myself more than I used to because I was so alone. I also learned to stop trying to tell people my story. They had their own problems.

There were times when I was left inside alone and hungry. There were days when I would wake up without my mom and nights I didn't sleep. I had to sit there and think of places where I thought she would go, and I would call and they would always say that she just left or wasn't there when I knew that she was right there.

I always had to cover for her to my grandma because she told us to. But what my mother didn't realize was that she was making a habit for me, because I always had to lie for her and say that she's in the bathroom or she went to the store. I used to hate that. I never felt comfortable telling my grandma the real story because she would come and get me and I would have to listen to her lecture about how my mom is no good. And when I would think about not telling my grandma the real deal, I thought I might be making my life worse. One time, we didn't have a phone. I think she did that on purpose so I wouldn't call when she left.

Sometimes I wished—God forgive me—that she was dead, just to know she was in a stable place. I would never have to call for her or wonder where she was because she would be six feet under the cement.

I can remember five good years when it seemed like we were going to make it. My mom was working, and she was able to buy a house on Tennessee Street in the Lower Ninth Ward. When she bought the house, everything was fine for a year and then she had got back into her habit when she met a man named Archie. She moved him into our house too fast, and they began to close the door of their room a lot. She had a job as a bartender and worked nights. One night she didn't come home. I began to think she wasn't even going to work sometimes. During the day, she started looking depressed—not cooking or talking to my Auntie Melva.

My brother Michael and I weren't always close, but we seemed to come together when times got hard. We began to suspect something was wrong because she kept closing her door. One afternoon, when she wouldn't respond, Mike started banging on the door.

"Ma, open the door!"

"Mike what do you want?"

I wanted to see, too. "Kesha, go to your room!" She was telling us to stop and Mike started picking the lock. He saw it in Archie's hand. He tried to flush it, but they got an argument. My mama started pushing my brother away, and he was asking, "Do you love me?" She didn't respond to him, and my brother started crying.

We heard my mom crying through the door. And when everything calmed down, Archie left. I went in and asked her about it. She said he was selling it. But then when she wasn't there, I found it under her mattress where she was sleeping and saw that it had already been used.

When I found it, it was an answer to myself. She came in late, and I wrote her a letter. She admitted she was doing it, but said she stopped. I asked her why she lied, and she said she didn't know. After we finished our conversation, I thought everything was going to be all right. That night, I slept in her bed, but when I woke up, she was gone. It seemed like a pattern all over again. I still think about her everyday.

MOVING

MAZANT STREET

FELICIANA STREET

GALVEZ STREET

NORTH TONTI STREET

NORTH MIRO STREET

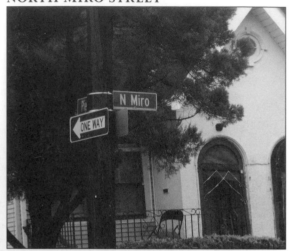

LOUISA STREET

INDEPENDENCE STREET

PILLAR TO POST

I have moved so many places growing up backwards and forwards from my grandma's house. I call myself a nomad because I have never had a stable place to live. My mother didn't make it too stable for me. Most kids would think it was fun to live in so many places, but I didn't like it one bit. I hated to move. I hated to meet new people and new children because I would have to start all over and learn how they are. My mom never let us know we were moving, she just packed up everything at the last minute, and we just left. My brothers used to whine when we were going to move, but my mom didn't pay attention.

All of the new houses never meant anything to me except for the house on Tennessee across the Industrial Canal in the Lower Ninth Ward. At the house on Tennessee, I had my own room, own space, and own privacy. I loved this house so much. I never wanted to leave it. I hoped this house would be in my family for my brothers and me to pass down the line. It represented my hope that my family would stay together. We only had it three and a half years, and then I moved back with my grandma.

It seemed no matter how many times I moved I always wound up at my grandma's pink house on the 3200 block of North Miro. To me that meant I was always welcome there. It felt like a home you would dream of. There were three meals a day, a room and everything.

TENNESSEE STREET

Meeting the people on my grandma's block was the best thing that ever happened to me because they're just like family. We became closer by having gatherings at each other's houses. The gatherings were times when everybody got together and had fun. All of the grown-ups would have their drinks and would dance with each other and sometimes with the kids. Everyone around the neighborhood was invited.

Our parties were so big everybody from other neighborhoods were coming. We had food that taste so good it made you want to smack yo mama. The drinks were so strong, you would leave walking sideways. Everybody talked about our parties because we would have so much fun.

LIVING WITH MY GRANDMA

I can always count on my grandma to provide a stable place for me. She cooks three meals a day and I eat every time plates go around. She's known for cooking and everybody comes over to eat, even neighbors. They all know how good her food is. Red beans get cooked every week, but gumbo gets cooked only on special occasions. I can't wait for holidays because I know she's going to cook it.

I asked my grandma, "How do you feel about me living here?" and she reminded me, "Kesha, you have always been with me. I feel like you're my child. Long as I have no problems, it's fine with me." She always says how hard her parents were on her, and she wants us to do right. I know she worries a lot about me. We had a lot of good times when I was small. We used to hang out every day. We went to Wal-Mart to get clothes and Krauss to get hair ribbons for me. When I came home from school, we'd sit in front of the TV to watch Maury at three o'clock. He always had interesting topics on his shows like disabled kids and unwed mothers, but there was no fighting like Jerry Springer or some of the other talk shows.

"I've always have been close with my grandchildren, even with the little ones coming up. I want my grandchildren to know me and to be around here. I look at a lot of people who don't take no time with their grandchildren and things, and you want these children to remember you. You're not going to be here always. They can always look back and say, 'Yeah, I remember my grandmother.' You know, cause my grandmother died when I was young and I remember how everybody used to come around and say things about me being young, I was about ten years old. I didn't have that much memory."

When I asked her about my mom, she said, "A mess." But then her heart softened a bit, "It was hard for me to accept when she got out there. It was real hard. I yelled at her and preached— I did everything I could. The only thing I do know is to be there for them. She says she loves her kids and she tells me that she loves me. I don't know. When a person gets caught out there in the world, I guess it's hard to get their life back together."

When I asked my grandma about whether she would feel comfortable with me writing about my mom she said, "I don't hide nothing from people — even neighbors. I let them know. Because I don't want you knockin on nobody's door for nothing. And don't have nothing to hide. I did what I was supposed to do for you. You ain't do what you were supposed to do for yourself."

When I was young, staying with my grandma was very hard because of her way of dealing with my mom. Sometimes my mom would pop up and call and say that she's depressed and hungry and my grandma would tell her no. Then later on in the day, I would hear her talking to someone on the phone about it. There were many times I'd cry because of the things she would say about my mom—not that she was lying, but just saying it repeatedly hurt and embarrassed me. Mike would just pretend not to listen and play his game. A few minutes later he would jump up and say, "I wish she'd shut up." I would just be sitting there waiting for a breakthrough, hoping for my life to get better.

My Aunt Melva and Grandma have a good relationship like a mother and daughter are supposed to. They're always together or on the phone. To me, they act like they're married. That's a good thing. It's something I always wished for with my mom.

I didn't realize my mom and Melva were so close until my grandma explained, "Until I had Melva, Pam was my only girl. I had the two boys and I guess I felt that she was the world to me. When Melva was born, people thought that was Pam's child. She took her everywhere she went. She took care of her. She loved Melva, and Melva misses her now as a sister because they were close. They were real close."

I asked her what she thought about me working on this book and she said, "I think it's nice, really nice. I was glad that you got into it. I'm proud of you, even though I be on you. But I do it for a reason. I know sometimes you think I'm being ugly with you or being too hard on you, but I have my reason why I do it. You gonna think about that way later on. Yeah, the older you get, that's when you realize. Whatever person goes through in life, it can help somebody else."

There were many times I would be sad waiting for my mother to come rescue me, but any time I really thought about it, I already was rescued. If it weren't for me staying with my grandma I don't know where I'd be.

Melva as a little girl.

INTERVIEW WITH MY GRANDMA ALINE ROBERTSON

My mom was from New Orleans and my dad is from the country. Torbert, Louisiana. It's a little, small country town. If you passed the street right here, you would have missed it. It's just a couple blocks.

My daddy was at Domino Sugar Refinery and my mother used to do day work. She cleaned houses. They had three children. Two girls and one boy. I'm the oldest. Aimena should be about two years under me. Henry was about three years under her. He's the baby.

We lived in a double house in the Seventh Ward. My mother lived on one side and my grandmother lived on the other side. It was a family house. You could go from one side to the other side through the kitchen. We had a nice big old backyard and all. It felt like a safe place to really live.

My grandmother didn't have to do too much for us. We had the school close to the neighborhood. We came home and went inside and did our little chores we had to do. I was always evil to the other kids. I took authority for a long time, and I made them listen to me, too. I liked doing that. I like being the boss. When my grandmother died, then my aunt moved on that side, and we could still always go from one side of the house to the other side.

THE NINTH WARD

We moved from the Seventh Ward when my mama bought her first house on Rocheblave. I guess I must have been about fifteen years old. People were saying, "It's bad in the Ninth Ward." We were scared and we didn't want to come in no Ninth Ward. I guess, too, we didn't want to leave our family. My mama had a large family and all the brothers would get together every weekend. There were family gatherings all the time, and when she moved, it meant that she was pulling away from that.

But once we moved, we started meeting people and found out it's no worse than nowhere else. I

19

mean, you live in your house. You're not out on the streets. You do what you have to do.

I met my first husband Roland when we first moved down here. I met his sister and her friends going back and forth to school. We had Roland Jr. in 1959 when I was seventeen. I was still at home with my mom and my dad. When I got pregnant, my daddy didn't have to tell me; I already knew that he don't take care of nobody and he ain't giving you nothing. He don't play that. He was very strict. My mom was a kind person; she'd help anybody. She'd do things, and not let him know. But if he find out, oh Lord. She's been deceased for a long time, and he's still the same, pretty much.

Roland signed for our son to be under his name, and we got married about a year later when I got pregnant with your mom. I thought he was the greatest, but he wasn't for me. He wasn't a person that wanted to work and take care of his family like he should have, so I had to do a lot of work. After having kids and all those responsibility was on me, and I didn't have any help, I said, "Well, you have to go." At that time it was hard. And you have to let your feelings go away and do what you have to do. And then after a while, it didn't hurt.

I met Nathan's father a couple of years later at my sister's house, and him and I got together and had my

son Nathan. He was a provider, but when he drink, he was crazy. That wasn't for me either.

After we couldn't make it, I moved back by my mom until I was able to get on my own and get my own place. I moved into the Florida Project on Bartholomew Street. At that time they had the big old porches and stuff. I mean, the people mostly worked, and when you came back home, you were inside. I had no problems at that time.

It wasn't what I would have done in life, but you know, I made a mistake. That's why I tell Kesha all the time, "You don't want to go that route." Cause you could only make it hard for yourself. Once you start having children, you gotta think about them. You have to provide for them, because a man may not be there always for their children.

I was lucky because my mom had stopped working. I used to take my kids over there in the morning before I went to work. After working in restaurants, I started working for the School Board because my kids and I were coming home and leaving home around the same time. You know, those other places you had to be at work at six o'clock, and I had nobody to bring me. I had to catch the bus.

I know how hard it is, and I tell Kesha all the time. All the time, I'm telling you, it's hard having all the responsibility on you. It's not nice, not everybody can make it. Talking about it and doing it is two different things. You gotta provide for. What you going to do, put them on your parents?

When you are dating, be careful for what you date, because you don't know how a person really is until you really get with them. They could turn your life upside down. I'm telling you, it's true. My mom never really talked, you know, like I think a parent or older people should tell their children to let them know what's going on.

MR. ROBINSON AND NORTH MIRO

I had been seeing Melvin Robinson around for a while. One night me and a girlfriend went out to the Cadillac bar off French Street and Prieur, and he told her he wanted to talk to me. She told me,

and we started talking. Then he left and went out of town and when he came back, we started dating. He started talking about us living together. I really wasn't willing to move in with him. But one day I was at work, and he rolled my furniture out of my house and into his house. He had to move me out. Out of the projects.

I was upset because I really liked it. I still tried to keep the apartment. We wanted to go back and put curtains up and stuff like that because if we don't make it, I'll always have me a place to stay. The lady over next door called the project people and told them I moved. I had to go turn in the key. Oh, was I mad! I was so mad. And that's how I got out of the projects.

I think Melva was about three or four years old when we got married. I know right before she started school, we changed her name. I didn't have to worry as much as before. It was a big relief.

We moved to North Miro after she started school. We were buying, you know, so it made it much easier. It was just a little home—one bedroom, kitchen, and bath on each side—but he knew how to do carpenter work. A lot of his family did carpenter work and he built a lot of houses with his daddy. It took him one month to renovate it. He did the work himself. When he got off work, he used to work up in here to two or three in the morning and then have to get right back up at six and go back to work. But he did it. He can still do this kind of work now. If something needs to be done, he'd do it himself.

FAMILY

I had no problem raising my kids. I really didn't. You know, Roland was the oldest and he was pretty much just like me. He took care of the rest of them. I always told him, if they did something wrong, he has to pay for what they did, too. So that made it all his job. Somebody has to be responsible.

UNCLE NATHAN

My Uncle Nathan is my grandmother's third child. He was a very talented man. He went to church every Sunday and didn't miss a bible study or church function at New Hope Baptist Church. He sung in the choir. He was a man of food and was known for his shrimp pasta. He was his own chef, and he had a food company called, "Just Like Mama's." Every Mardi Gras he would be under the bridge on Claiborne and Orleans in the Sixth Ward selling his most famous pasta. Everyone would be in a huge crowd, which they called a line, waiting to get some.

Before he made his career in cooking he was in the army for thirteen years and received various medals and awards and from there on he was a veteran in the Gulf War.

He was separated from his first wife Michelle—whom he had a child with in 1987—after he went to the army. He was remarried in 1996 to Tamika Kent. Everyone knew that Tamika wasn't good for him but when you're in love there are some things you don't see until you're ready to see it. Her bad ways were noticeable to everyone except him. She always put him out when they fussed and tell him harsh things like, "Don't come back!" Everyone saw that she was selfish and all she worried about was herself, but he was just too blind to see it. Still he always took care of Lil' Nathan.

My relationship with my Uncle Nathan wasn't as strong as it could have been. We only had a typical uncle and niece relationship when he was telling me what not to do. It was never a time where we sat down and laughed about something we enjoyed or reviewed what I wanted to do in life.

He began taking trips backwards and forwards to the doctor. He was diagnosed with cancer and he also had a tumor in his brain.

My grandma's oldest child Roland had already died, but I thought it was going to be my mom next because of her drug addiction. I never thought it was going to be my Uncle Nathan. I never looked behind the active things he did until the doctors said he had less than six months to live. Everyone was in denial that he was sick. My grandma remembers, "They said there was nothing else they could do for him. They had been saying he was going to die. I didn't believe it—they don't know what they're talking about, he's going to be all right. I'll make sure you take your medicine, make sure you eat, make sure you have your juice and you'll be all right." No one could believe it because he was always happy cooking and singing. It was a shock to the family to see a person have to put down their responsibilities and goals to lay in a sick bed.

He wasn't getting along with Tamika, and at times she would put him out. He moved in with my grandma. She reflects, "It was his decision, not mine, and that's what counts. I didn't tell him, but I wouldn't turn him down either. That's my child. I didn't interfere with his marriage. He made his decision. His wife was a good person, but she was kinda hot-headed. Maybe they weren't getting along and he would come home, and she didn't like it."

As time passed he got worse and worse. He was loosing weight every day, and he would lose his self strength to do things for his self. His voice was cracking and you couldn't hear anything when he tried to talk. We had to make flash cards to know what he was saying.

My grandma wasn't taking things very well to see her son slowly dying. As far as me, I tried to be there any way I could because I knew my help was needed. My grandma reflects, "When a person is sick, you gotta be dedicated to them, which can be hard when you are trying to work, too. A lot of times at home

when I just wanted to just do something or go somewhere, I really couldn't go because I had to be here with him. I kinda like put my life on hold for a little while. I was still able to go, but not freely, like to stay for hours and hours, you know. Kesha really helped me good, she really did. She used to help him better than me. I'd say, 'Kesha, I'm going to the store, I'm going shopping. Will you stay with him?' She never said no, that was a great help to me."

"I gave him a bell he could ring, so we could hear it. And he rang that bell. When he rang that bell, you better hurry up and get there. He used to like the door closed. He was more of a private person, and I think he was feeling cold a lot. When you'd open up that door, he'd knock you out with the heat. He'd look and you and say, 'What took you so long?' I'd say, 'Baby, I was in the bathroom,' or something. 'Well, it was too long. What you got? What you got to eat?' He loved banana ice cream on a stick. And oh did he love the candy and cookies. We kept all of that for when he wanted it, and all different types of juice."

"He was the type of person, I don't care what you fix, if he didn't feel like eatin it, he ain't gonna eat that. 'I don't want that. I want something else.'"

He didn't like leftovers either. I was only fifteen years old and had seen many things I shouldn't have. It hurt me to see a death coming along.

He died before Thanksgiving of 2003 on Friday November 14th. He lived more than three times as long as the doctors predicted. That morning, he was trying to tell me something. I talked to my grandma about it and she said, "He was trying to tell me something too, but I had to go to work. I said, 'Kesha, please go in there and go see what he's talking about.' He just kept on pointing. I said, 'I don't understand what you're trying to tell me baby.'"

I wondered what was over there and then remembered a picture of him and Tamika. I don't know if he wanted us to call her.

Everyone shared their tears and sympathy, which was good to see who cared, but it was still a big emp-ty spot in my grandma's heart that her second child was gone. He died in the front room of my grand-ma's house where I sleep now. A lot of people think I should be scared, but I'm only being protected in that room.

At the funeral his wife and kids sat on the other side of the church like we were enemies or some-thing. But when his wife Tamika received the American flag from the Army, she broke down and put it in my grandma's hands. As days passed we all got closer to Tamkia and Lil' Nathan, which is all Nathan wanted, but I wish it didn't happen after he died. My Grandma tells me, "We talk, she'll call and see how I'm doing. But I guess when you're younger, you don't understand."

AUNT MELVA

Melva is my mom's little sister, and she's also the baby of my grandma's kids. When I was small, I used to be with Melva all the time. She brought me everywhere she went. One time she even had me at one of her slumber parties. I've seen a picture of all of her friends surrounding me, with our thumbs up for the camera.

Melva made me do things for her. Everything she wanted out of the kitchen she told me to go and get it. If I came back with the wrong thing she would fuss at me and I would get mad and try to get away from her. I always felt a need to be with her. She was like a big sister because all I had was two broth-ers, and I was the only girl. If I wasn't with Melva, I was all alone with those two aggravating brothers of mine.

She and my mom got along well when my mother wasn't high. On a regular day they used to hang out and go shopping and talk all day, but the beautiful part about their friendship is when they laugh. I guess that made them closer day by day. They'd talk on the phone for hours at a time. I could hear my mother laugh from my room and I would know who she was on the phone with laughing like that. Then Melva would come by our house and we'd wind up going some place and stay out for hours. My mother would leave and get high again.

When I asked Melva why she thought my mom used drugs she said, "To some extent I think self-esteem plays a part in it. She spent a period of just going through different relationships with people. Being involved with people who didn't necessarily have their life together. They put their bad weight down on her, and forced her to do a lot of things that she didn't really need to get involved in. Just being at the wrong place, wrong time, wrong type of company."

Before my Uncle Nathan died my grandma, Melva, and I were taking care of him every step of the way. Melva would come and sit with him while I was at school, then I would sit with him when my grandma wasn't at home. "Taking care of Uncle Nathan wasn't the easiest thing to do because that's the youngest boy of the family. He's the second brother that we had to watch go through a terminal illness. It was hard because at one point in life they are full of energy. They are vibrant. Life was going great for him as far as him being interactive in church and volunteering. He loved to cook. He loved to talk. It was a hard struggle. A person that normally goes to the bathroom and does everything for themselves is now at a point where they need people to change their diapers, and feed them."

At the time, she was pregnant with her second child and was doing what she could do day by day. "There were some instances when I took him out. He wanted to go to the bank and get some money and take care of his monthly expenses. His body was so fragile, he fell down. I was pregnant at that time; it was hard for me to pick him up. I was at a point where I wanted to cry, because I could hardly keep him up myself."

Melva had her second child, Teyond, a week after Uncle Nathan died. A month later, she was pregnant with her third child. Now she's trying to get her career back on track. She says, "I wish that I had went forward with completing college, and then had the kids after. It's a lot harder to juggle kids and school at the same time. Now I've got two younger ones, I've got to get them to the point where they're in school so I can go back to school. But it's interesting to watch kids grow up. They say the darndest things. Even though they are so small, my kids have such great intelligence. It's a great period to just watch them grow."

I asked her why she thought women in our family did most of the caretaking. She said, "I think a lot of times men don't want to step up to the role of dealing with sickness and stuff like that. When Nathan was sick, the only person that took care of him that was a male was his father. He came every now and then with some things. It's hard for some men to deal

with. Most of the time women are so used to taking care of children that a mothering instinct comes in. I think it's a lot easier for a woman to step in and take the responsibility of taking care of someone that's sick and needs the help." What happens when you haven't been taught or don't have a mothering instinct? "You've got to realize that at some point in your life you may need someone to help you. When you do, a great deal of emotion and sympathy goes in. If your heart is full, you just go forward."

For the last few months, Melva, her husband and kids have discovered a new and improved relationship with God and have been attending Evergreen Missionary Baptist Church. Now that she doesn't have a job on Sunday she gets to be where God is.

INTERVIEW WITH MY MOM

Kesha: Mother, what is your full name?

Pam: My name is Pamela Ann Mack.

K: Where did you grow up?

P: I grew up in New Orleans, Louisiana, in the Lower Ninth Ward.

K: What school did you go to?

P: I went to Locket Elementary. From Locket to Carver to Nicholls Senior High.

K: What was it like?

P: Locket was fun. I was young. It was a lot of playing around, meeting new people every year. Middle school was exciting. High school was some problems.

K: What were the problems?

P: My problems was I really didn't want to go to school.

K: Did you finish?

P: I went all the way up to the 12th grade and I didn't participate in the graduation.

K: Did you get your diploma?

P: No, I never I went back to get my diploma.

K: What did your parents do for a living?

P: First my mother was a nursing assistant. She left from working at Charity Hospital to work for the public school board.

K: How long did she work there?

P: She was over twenty-two years with the school board.

K: How old were you when you got pregnant?

P: My first child?

K: Yes.

P: I had my first child when I was twenty years old.

K: How old are all of your children?

P: My oldest son, Rodney Mack, is twenty four, my youngest son Michael Jackson is nineteen and my daughter is sixteen.

K: When did you start your habit?

P: I started my habit when I was twenty years old. Matter of fact, my habit started long before twenty because I first started drinking alcohol.

K: Around what age?

P: I started drinking alcohol when I was sixteen. And I went from drinking to smoking marijuana.

K: How did you get involved in that?

P: Marijuana?

K: Mmhm.

P: With friends.

K: School friends?

P: School friends, boyfriends.

K: What was it like?

P: It felt good. I was mellow, you know, cool. Everything was funny to me when I was smoking marijuana.

K: Was it peer pressure?

P: Well, I had a lot of peer pressure on me because I had a lot of problems with my mom that I couldn't deal with so I used drugs and alcohol to escape.

K: What was the problems with your mama?

P: My mom believed in her boyfriend. She just didn't know how to relate with me. She didn't know how to show me love. Because I was the only girl, I felt neglected in a lot of ways and so I was searching for love in all the wrong places.

K: After all of that, after you had your kids and everything, were you still involved in drugs when you had your second pregnancy?

P: Well, on my second pregnancy I was married and I never went into straight years of getting loaded, I always, you know—

K: Off and on?

P: It was off and on. It was only when I got depressed or something like that, that I used.

K: Did you change from marijuana to something else?

P: Yes, I did. I went from marijuana to click-ems, and from click-ems to crack. I started smoking crack when I was twenty years old.

K: What are click ems?

P: It's marijuana dipped into some kind of juice.

K: I never heard of that.

P: Don't worry about it. I started smoking crack—well, it was called cocaine then. We used to call it free-basing.

And I started free-basing. From that day—the first day that I used I can say that it was an addiction. It was like I found my drug addiction. You know, the alcohol wasn't it—

K: As good as that was...

P: Right, it wasn't like I had to drink everyday. It wasn't that I had to smoke weed everyday, but when I started smoking cocaine, it was a difference. It was like *wow*—it was like the thing that helped me block away all my problems. I didn't feel nothing. I didn't feel nobody else's feelings, you know. It was all about just doing what I was doing and it was like my problems was taken away from me. But then when I didn't smoke, then I felt all my problems.

K: After all your kids was born and everything like that, when did you start leavin em inside?

30

P: I started leaving them inside when they was old enough.

K: Around what age?

P: How old were you when I started leavin you inside?

K: From what I remember I was about—how old you be in the fourth grade?

P: You was in the fourth grade when I left y'all inside?

K: Yeah, we was on Miro Street in that green and yellow house. How old I was then?

P: Oh.

K: Seven, should be? Michael, nine or ten.

P: Well, let me tell you like this: I don't know exactly when it happened, but I do know that if I started using and I didn't want y'all to see me, I would leave. You know, I would leave. I never wanted to look direct in y'all face so…I never really…I never leave y'all unless I felt as though one of y'all was about to get up, and then I had to leave, you know.

And then when I left, and if I didn't stop or if I felt I looked too bad, I just wouldn't come back, you know. I knew at one point that y'all would go right down the street by your Maw Maw or that y'all would call her and let her know that I'm not there and she will come down and get y'all so then I knew—I felt that y'all was okay. And so I just didn't come back. I was embarrassed, I was hurting, and stuff like that.

K: So how did you used to feel when you would lie to us?

P: I felt bad, you know. I never did like to lie to you

all and that's one thing that I always instilled in y'all to just be honest, but I used to lie so I could continue doin what I was doin, you know.

K: How did you think we feel—how do you think we felt when you used to lie?

P: Well, I knew that y'all was hurt and I knew that y'all knew that I was lying. One thing about it is that you all can look in my face and tell when I'm lying because we had honesty with each other. We always had a very good communication. And that was the way I wanted me and my kids because me and my brothers and sisters, we never did. So, anytime any one of us lied to each other we knew it.

K: So when you used to be gone, and I used to be calling for you, how did you used to feel?

P: It used to hurt, you know, because I never wanted to send you through any hard feelings or—I never, I made a promise when you was born and I let the promise go—and this is bringing back a lot of feelings [crying]…

K: It's okay. Sometimes when I used to call you, you used to be right there.

P: Mmhm.

K: Most of the time.

P: Well, you used to call where?

K: By what that man name?

P: Who? Well, Kesha, you know a lot of times when you, your Maw Maw, when any one of y'all called me, if I was using, I wouldn't answer the phone because I knew y'all wanted me to come home. At the time, once you start using drugs, it's not like you're just gonna to put it down, or say, "This is enough." You know, you go into it and say I'm going to smoke one and one always wind up to a thousand or more. And by me being a drug addict, it was hard for me. It was very hard for me to say, "Okay well, I'm finished." And before I lie to you, I'll let somebody else lie and say that I'm not there, because I knew you wouldn't understand me saying, "I'm coming, I'm coming, I'm coming," and I know that I'm not coming. You know, I didn't want to lie to you, but then it was like you kept calling, or whatever, and you left me no other choice but to lie to you. It was like you knew anytime I stayed out after twelve o'clock I was getting loaded.

K: Mmhm. How do you think we felt when you left for days?

P: I knew you all were hurt. I knew after being gone for just maybe two hours that two hours was too long away. You know, especially when y'all don't know where I'm at. If y'all don't know where I'm at, y'all know I'm getting loaded.

K: You used to know that we used to be inside sometimes hungry?

P: Y'all could have fixed something to eat, but y'all didn't want to.

K: No! Without groceries.

P: Oh, well, yeah.

K: How did you feel that time when Archie was staying with us and I had asked you was you was using again. And you told me no, and y'all had gotten into that big fight—you, Archie and Mike?

P: Oh, I didn't like that. I didn't like that at all. I felt real, real hurt, but I was lying because I didn't want you to know, and I was doing good at the time and it was like just because this person came into my life it was like, it was a big change, and I knew I had let y'all down, and I knew y'all was hurting. I didn't like it at all, and I didn't like the fact that Michael was banging the door open, and stuff like that. He invaded my privacy—regardless. Regardless of what I was doing, he knew what was going on so he shouldn't have been forcing his way into my room.

K: Well, you didn't used to close your door, so—

P: But the point is that I am still the adult. [I know] I'm still the mama. And if I, regardless of if I'm doing wrong, if I'm doing what's right, it is my choice to shut my door, and he was wrong for violating that. You know, because he had no right. And supposing if he would have caught the pipe up at my mouth—imagine how he would have made me feel. You know, it was enough that I was using, but I never could have you or him seeing me do this, you know, it could have drove me crazy. I'm not saying he was wrong—well, yes, I am saying that he was wrong. And I'm not making myself be right for doing what I was doing, but he was wrong to take it that far.

K: We also knew what you was doing when you closed your door because you know how you said we always had an honest relationship and everything, and we would know something was wrong when you closed the door.

P: That's why whenever I shut any door in my house I had to have a problem out of you or Michael, even if I went into the bathroom and shut the door for a long time. Yeah.

K: When your mama found out you was using?

P: My mama found out I was because I stayed gone for two weeks. She was hurt, you know, she couldn't understand why, you know. I tried to explain it to her, and I tried to get her to go to some meetings and I tried to let her know that a lot of my childhood things led me to it. I am not as strong as you are. You are a very strong young lady.

K: Why did you used to get depressed?

P: Okay, a lot of reasons why I used to get depressed was because I always wanted to have and receive everything that y'all wanted, and by me being a single parent, and I was always working, and y'all had to have what ever it was y'all wanted. I would give up light money, telephone money, rent money, when y'all said you needed this and that. I'd just go off and spend it and then I be behind, you know, with bills. I work and I work and I work and I tried to keep everything up, and then at one point, I would get stressed to where I needed some time for me.

I think my main issue was that I hated the fact that I was a single parent. I felt as though I should have had a husband, or I should have kept my husband, you know, where I could have help with you all. But, it was a lot of things that happened between him and I— he was also using, and when I had made a decision to stop using, he wasn't ready so then I had to take on my responsibilities by myself, and that was y'all having everything y'all needed and wanted.

I think a lot of times I felt guilty about the times when I was using, so when I was clean and sober I tried to give y'all everything I could, you know, to make up for the things that I didn't give y'all when

I was using, and I was killing myself. Because, you know, y'all was taking advantage of it. You know, I think y'all knew that I was guilty, and that I would go out of my way to do this and that. And y'all would just, "Look I want to get this tennis shoe, I want to get this here." And you know, I was like, I couldn't say no. You know, I couldn't say no because of the simple fact I messed up a lot myself. I felt like "Well, hey, compared to what I messed up, buying y'all what y'all wanted wasn't no problem." But deep down inside, it was putting me back, you know.

K: So, this is the type of thing that drove you to where you wanted to kill yourself?

P: Well, I wanted to kill myself because I was unhappy with myself. I never liked the fact that I was a drug user. I had a lot of issues as far as with my family, you know, and I could never understand why. So, the communication I made with my kids, that's the main reason I installed it into you all, that no matter what happens, no matter what we go through that we never change on each other, because we all going to go through something. Just like you—I wish the best for you, and I hope and pray that you don't have to go through what I went through, but you will go through something, and I just want to be there for you. You know, whether it's right or whether it's wrong, I'ma be there. As long as I'm clean and sober, I can. But when I use, I know I can't.

K: So how many programs have you been in?

P: I've been in treatment centers practically, Kesha you would say, all my life. I think I really had a mental problem that should have been taken care of. And I told my mama that when I was really young that I really felt as though I needed to see psychiatrist because I had a depression problem since I was young. I think that was one of my problems or why I kept doing the same thing over and over and expecting different results and nothing ever changed.

K: How did the programs help you—or did they help you at all?

P: Of course they did. They helped me a lot. They helped me to change a lot. They helped me build up my self-esteem, because I have very, very low self-esteem. I thought about myself but I put myself down a lot also. You know, I always felt like I could have been better or I could have done this or I could have done that. And today I found out that my life was already planned—you know what I'm saying, I just needed to make the right choices. And at the time, I was always making the wrong choices. And I made the wrong choices because I never really took the time out to evaluate my feelings or what I wanted to do. So, today I learned that you have to take the time and you have to make the right choices for yourself. And God is with me at all times, you know, I just need to make the right choices to give praises and make the right choices to make my life easier.

K: Which one of the programs was the best before the Turning Point?

P: Before Turning Point, Salvation Army. Salvation Army—that was my best program.

K: What was Salvation Army like?

P: I enjoyed it. At first I thought I wasn't going to like it because it was not only just a drug rehab program, but it was a shelter for homeless people and in the program we had to help out the homeless. And that was the most wonderful experience that I have ever had because, you know, coming up we used to look at homeless people [mmhm] like something was wrong with em or they did something, you wouldn't have anything to do with them. When I was at Salvation Army, I was like a leader there. I found a lot of love in the homeless people. I found that some people just love to be around a lot of people. You know, they're not all just homeless people. Everybody had their own reasons for being there. There was a lot of smart, intelligent people, you know what I'm saying? And Kesha, when I experienced that, reaching out to them, it helped me to know that somebody had to reach out to me so I had to reach out to somebody, you know what I'm sayin?

And there's nothing wrong with loving everybody. It helped me because I used to look down on some people. And you know, God didn't like that, I know He didn't, and so I had to get to that point of reaching out and helping others, because when I needed help I expected my help from anywhere. You know, just help me. Somebody help me, you know.

Today, I help and I do it from my heart. I have unconditional love for everyone, you know what I'm saying. At the house where I'm at now, you know, people come in straight from the street. And I have stuff put in a locker for people who don't have. I have my own locker, but I have a locker with food, with sheets, with towels, with every thing—soap powder, you know Everything that any lady could use I have in that locker to give to somebody who don't have anything.

K: Why did you get involved in this program?

P: I looked at your eyes and I knew that you were sick and tired of me at that point and I knew that I had to do something. But, matter of fact, not just because of you but I was sick and tired myself. I had been beating myself down to the ground. And I had never gotten to the point and it was an experience for me, but I just put my hands up and I said, "God, I surrender—please." I came to Turning Point and I met Mr. Robert and he is the most wonderful man—he has so much love and so much understanding. The love that he have helps you learn to love yourself and love others, and helps you to get out of here. You know, it's a lot of love.

K: Do you enjoy it?

P: I love it. I love it—I really do. I love it so much that I never really want to come back to New Orleans, you know like Thanksgiving and my birthday? I got depressed because I wanted to be with you. I didn't really want to come to New Orleans. But I decided to be with you. I just want to be with my daughter. You know, my daughter ain't want me around. When I call her I can't talk to her, you know what I'm saying? It was driving me crazy because I thought that you had given up on me.

And I know you think, "Well, Kesha is doin her own thing. Kesha have her life. Kesha has to be responsible because you wasn't responsible enough to be there for her." I wasn't looking at it like that. You know, I was looking at it wrong. Oh, I did it this time, my daughter don't want to be bothered with me, and so I was very depressed, and all I really needed to do was see you.

K: How has the Turning Point changed you?

P: It showed me that I needed to go closer to God and change my attitude towards life. It changed my attitude towards women, it changed my attitude to-wards the world. I always had a problem with women, and now it's like I'm living in a household with fifteen women. I used to say things to hurt women feelings. A lot of women were jealous of me because of my boldness, because of my straightforwardness, and strongness that's in me that I never saw was in me. A lot of people see it in people, and before they like me, they'll find something against me and so I never could really get close to women. But today, you know, these women over here acknowledge and want what they have. Every time I speak, I touch one of their hearts or help them out in some kind of way.

K: Do you plan on being sober for the rest of your life?

P: I plan on being sober for the rest of my life.

K: Now, overall, everything that you have gone through, do you love yourself more?

P: I love myself. I love myself so much.

K: Well, that is all.

PART II:
WOMEN IN MY NEIGHBORHOOD

I live in the biggest neighborhood in New Orleans, the Ninth Ward, which is way down from the city, like at the bottom. It used to be a cypress swamp until the early part of the 1900s when the railroad tracks started to cut through the area. In the 1920s, the Industrial Canal was built through the neighborhood and the lower part is now called the Lower Ninth, or the CTC, which can stand for Cross the Canal or Cut Throat City. Driving around, you can see a lot of development and businesses related to that Canal.

In the 1940s, streets were created and public utilities expanded. The area was home to both white and black families. It was one part of the city where black people could buy houses. They felt safer from the world because most of the people were similar to them and living the same kind of lifestyle. For many years the Ninth Ward was a picture of stability, with strong black families in homes that many of them owned. In the 1950s, the Desire and Florida Public Housing Complexes opened, too, which provided low-income housing. People from all over the city started moving down to the Ninth Ward to live in the complexes.

In the 1960s, New Orleans chose to begin public school desegregation in my part of the Ninth Ward at William Frantz Elementary. Many people have prob-

ably heard of the story of Ruby Bridges. She was the first black girl to attend that school. The white parents started taking their children out of school because they didn't want them around her. They said that if the black girl had to stay, then they wouldn't anymore. They spit on Ruby, threw stuff at her and she had to go to school with bodyguards. After awhile, some of the white parents started sending their children back to the school. But it didn't last long because they started moving away.

When I went to Frantz Elementary I was in the second grade. Ruby Bridges came back to pay a visit to the school. We all thanked her and said, "2, 4, 6, 8. Who do we appreciate? Ruby! Ruby! We love you!" All of the children were saying that, but I don't think there were any white kids.

Today, the Ninth Ward is predominantly black. Families grow and learn about each other. The men join the military or do carpentry work. They work offshore and some of them are foremen on the riverfront. The women may sit with the elderly, do house cleaning and work at hotels. A lot of children try to move away from the Ninth Ward if they can, so there are a lot of older people here.

Women play a big part in the neighborhood. They communicate with each other by watching over everyone. They run barrooms that act as home bases, and go to church together, worshiping the same God. They organize Nights Out Against Crime, have participated in political organizations like the Black Panthers, and joined social clubs like the Nine Times Social and Pleasure Club. They take care of the community and each other while juggling their losses and responsibilities. These are some of their stories.

INTERVIEW WITH HELEN FREY

I have known Mr. and Mrs. Frey my whole life. Mrs. Frey is from "little Napoleonville" and Mr. Frey was from the St. Bernard Projects in the Seventh Ward. Mrs. Frey moved to New Orleans in 1958 to go to school at University of New Orleans. Her aunt's husband had a nephew that he wanted her to meet. "That's how I met Mr. Frey. We got married in 1960." In the late 1970s, they bought their house in the Ninth Ward.

The Freys live three houses to the left from mine and have always been nice people to my family. They were at my christening and Mr. Frey always called me his godchild. Mrs. Frey explains why: "My husband is really not her godfather, but the person who was supposed to christen her was late and I told Mr. Frey to come and stand in for him." I sure wished that he could have been my godfather because I haven't talked to my real *parrain* for years. I always thought of Mr. Frey as my godfather anyway. He had cookies and freeze pops for my brothers and me every day we came home from school. We've grown up, but Mr. Frey would still be in the door laughing with cookies for us. Mrs. Frey says, "Every time we get something, 'Did you give Kesha some?' I tell him, 'Kesha doesn't like that. She's a big girl now.' But he still thinks of her as his little girl."

One day around Thanksgiving 2004, Mr. Frey was really sick. and was admitted to the hospital. He

was having heart problems and they told Mrs. Frey that he didn't have too long to live. She didn't pay them any mind because she knew in her heart that he was going to get better. Mr. Frey laid in that sick bed and fought for his life. After a month, they sent him home, but within a week he was back.

Around this time, I did an interview with Mrs. Frey for this book. It was hard for her to concentrate because she was so worried about him. She didn't know what else to do except to pray. A few days later, I went to see him at Baptist Hospital to bring him some flowers. Family members were standing around looking at him laying there covered in white sheets with wires and things hooked up to him. His daughter was sitting next to him holding his hand. We gazed into his face. It was quiet except for the beep of the heart monitor every five seconds. It hurt deeply, like our hearts were getting destroyed by a shredder. I couldn't take it anymore to see such a beautiful person suffer so badly.

December 20, 2004 Mr. Frey died of heart failure. It was a difficult day for everyone. I was so hurt, I couldn't make it to the funeral. I still haven't been able to pay my proper respects to Mrs. Frey. I want to comfort her and just say how sorry I am for what happened, but I don't know what got into me, I don't know how to say it. Every day I think about telling her I'm sorry, but I just don't have to the guts to do it. I want to tell her how much their family's care meant to me and that Mr. Frey will always be my godfather.

BEGINNINGS

I grew up in Napoleonville, Louisiana. I'm one of six kids. My mother and father were strict, real strict. We had to do everything by the book. The town was about sugarcane and that's about it. My father worked at a sugar refinery and my mother was a nurse at Napoleonville Clinic. After she stopped working at the hospital, she worked for a private family until my dad took sick and she quit. I really only went into nursing because I always wanted to work with kids. I was a nurse's aide at Southern Baptist Hospital, and then I became a supervisor in the nursery. Later, I went to housework. You know, a nanny, and that's what I'm doing now. The family I work for is in Metairie. I've been working for them for ten years. I was with the parents before the kids

were born. They really grew up with my grandkids, and they're just like my grandkids. The little boy's seven now, and my grandson is five, so they're together.

THE NINTH WARD

I was Uptown for a long time. In the late 1970s, my husband said, "We're going to buy a house downtown." I really didn't want to come down here because I heard so much about it. I used to hear about a lot of murder, breaking in, and raping, and none of the good stuff.

When I moved, the block only had three families. We were the first. The rumors were not true. It's just like Napoleonville. In Napoleonville, everybody's kin to each other—everybody's cousins whether you knew them or not. Mamas are auntie, and that's how it is down here. Everybody here is the same. Now all the kids call me Mama Frey or Mrs. Frey. If they're on the porch and you go inside, you say, "Good evening." You just don't see sugarcane.

But you do see pecans. And if you want to see oranges, you can go in my backyard. My husband asks, "If you wanted to go somewhere, where would you go?" I said, "Right here." I won't move from my neighborhood. I love it.

When the kids were smaller, I used to love to see them out playing and being together, and my husband used to like to take pictures. He used to take weddings pictures and all that. Birds, bees, anything. We used to have parties. It was just a family, and we would invite the neighbors and anybody that wanted to come. Mr. Frey would get in the backyard and cook. He had his barbeque pit, and he'd be making jambalaya. He used to walk our three German Shepherd dogs. He was real active until his heart gave him problems and he had to stop. You know, he couldn't breathe too good, or walk fine.

I worry about people from the outside. The outsiders come in and try to sell things, what are they selling out here? Sometimes they meet on the corner. The ones that grew up around here don't worry me. Some of the guys that hang out were small kids when I first moved. "Hi, Mrs. Fry." "Hi neighbor." Or whatever. I would never let them in my house, but...

When I first moved here, I did have a break-in, but it wasn't anyone off of this street. It's a long story and a scary story if you think of it. My youngest son was a teenager. He came in and found two girls in the house. One was taking a bath and one was making sandwiches. And the one that were making the sandwich ran. He locked the one that was taking a bath in the bathroom. He called his dad, and his dad called the policeman, and the policeman came.

I had one of the little portable televisions, and a telephone on the counter, brand-new that wasn't out of the box—they didn't take that. They went into my daughter's room and took all her things. She was getting ready for her prom, and they took her dress. They must have been in here all day. I mean, took a *bath*. They were pretending that they were living here. She was just an ordinary girl, just like Kesha and everybody else.

My husband, the lover of children, didn't press charges or anything, because they were kids. They talked to them instead, and didn't press charges. But I wanted to, and I bet I would have. I just wanted them to learn a lesson.

My daughter was so scared, and I think that's what made her want to go to military. She said, "I don't know want to live in New Orleans." And this is the only place she had been. I love the three of them equal, but my daughter is my daughter, my sister, my friend, and my mother. She's a sergeant, master sergeant. She's stationed in Turkey right now. We've been to visit her in Germany and gone to Paris and Amsterdam

MR. FREY

Right now, I'm going through a bad time because my husband is in the hospital. He has heart problems, and they wanted to have him go on kidney dialysis, and he's refusing it. And I'm a basket case right now because all the doctors told me to do was come home and get my black dress out. It's so hard after forty-five years of marriage. I think he's giving up. You know, he has so much illness.

I don't know whether this is a good day or a bad day coming in. Yesterday I was talking with him on the telephone, he was fine. I told him, "She's coming to do an interview." He's conscious of everything—that's why I can't make a decision for him because he is conscious and he aware of everything that's going on. But he has a bad heart. In fact, he don't have a heart, they say, just a string of it. The medicine that they gave him for his heart messed up his kidney.

Doctors are just so blunt. They just tell you what's going to happen. And it's not bad in a way—they don't have you just sitting there thinking something else. He told me he said, "Mrs. Frey if you don't get him, this is his last week. That's it." I'm going to get my priest to talk to him tomorrow, and see what he's going to say.

My daughter talks to him every day. He said to leave him alone. It's his body, he can make up his own mind. His sister was on it, and she stayed on it ten years, and she lived a happy life until the end. You know, she started getting sick. And I said, "Go on it." I don't know what's going to happen.

Forty-five years, and he and I have been in this house just the two of us unless my daughter comes home on leave. But he and I have been right here together. And we were very happy. You know, if I don't go there, he won't see nobody but me. By the time I get in, "Where's Helen?"

Maybe when my husband will be here, he can have you over here all day. Kesha knows, he loves to talk. And something for school, like when I told him she was there, he said, "Oh, I wish I was there." He encourages kids. He tells my grandchildren, "You can't get by unless you read. I don't care what you read, read." I tell him, "You need to go on Jeopardy." He's really smart.

INTERVIEW WITH
JANALYN MOORE JOHNSON

I've known Ms. Jan since I was small because my Aunt Melva went to school with her daughter Krissy. Every time Krissy and Melva would get together, I would always be with Melva. Every time they saw me, they asked about the bump on my pinky that looks like an extra little finger. They'd say, "Girl, you still got that thing?" And I would say, "Yeah." They would laugh and play with it.

Krissy had two little girls Timberlyn and Timbrielle that were going to the same school as me in elementary school. They were younger than me and I used to watch them at school and walk them home in the afternoon. Whenever I would go outside, I'd watch them while they were playing. It felt good to know I was the boss, and whatever I said goes. If I told them to hop or skip, they had to do it or they would be punished at home for not listening to me. But I never took advantage of being the boss and made them do things just to do it. I took care of them like they were my own and used to say they were my little sisters.

If anything went wrong, they ran to me and I taught them not to be scared. Sometimes when we played in the park, some other little girls on bikes would circle around Timberlyn and Timbrelle. One day, Timberlyn tried to get out of the circle, but the other girls wouldn't let her. She called for me, but I

didn't hear her because I was so high on the swing—swinging away trying to reach the sky.

Timberlyn stopped calling for me, she just jumped out of the circle to a hard fall on the ground. When I heard that cry, I jumped off the swing and ran to her trying to find out what happened. She cried and cried until I was able calm her down. She told me that the little girls were trying to trap her and tried to run over her with their bikes. The head of them yelled, "No, we didn't!"

"Yes, you did!" Timberlyn said.

"You lying ugly self!" said the girl.

Angry, Timberlyn walked over to her saying repeatedly, "Yes, you did." The girl got off the bike with her hands balled up and just as I was getting up to pull Timberlyn back, the little girl hit her and the lick just passed on. When I finally broke them up, I brought Timberlyn and Timbrielle home.

The next day when I brought them home from school, Ms. Jan said that she wanted to talk to me. When I got in the house, she sat me down and asked me if I had been making her granddaughters fight in the park. I said no and explained about the day before. She told me that from now on, she was going to be picking them up and that my work wasn't needed anymore. I was so heartbroken, but we all still seemed to stay close. I saw her just about every day when school let out and when my grandparents had parties. She was smiling all the time, would give me a hug, and ask me how I was doing. I didn't know that she invented a game called Kangaroo Court that taught children how to deal with conflict.

Kesha: Where did you grow up?

Jan: My first years were in the Desire Project. I attended Moton Elementary School, I went to Lockeed Cohen Junior High School, and I graduated from Nicholls in 1974.

K: Ok. What was your childhood like?

J: It had it's good times and it's bad times. It was kinda tough.

K: Care to describe?

J: My father died when I was 12 years old—it was a really tough time for me. That was the first time I ever tried to commit suicide.

K: What did you feel like?

J: You can't describe a loss like that. I never lost a child, but when you feel like you've lost the only person that loves you in your life, it's just kind of devastating.

K: When you tried to commit suicide, what was your thought?

J: Well, I knew from church that I wasn't supposed to because I would go to hell. But, I felt that I was

already living in hell and it couldn't be much worse and that God would understand, and He would put me with my daddy anyway.

K: Well, how did you get over that stage?

J: It's not that was the only time I tried. I tried several different times throughout my life. But after my husband died in '87, I knew I couldn't do it because my children would be parentless. So I didn't attempt it anymore.

K: What was their father like?

J: I remember giving him a trophy for father of the year. We were stationed at an Air Force Base in the Phillipines. He loved to travel, but I didn't like traveling that much. I was more into education, and into making rank. He was from Boston. He played basketball for Boston College. He died of a massive heart attack in 1987 when we were stationed in Japan. He was playing basketball. I was twenty-nine and he was thirty-four. My kids were six, nine, and twelve.

K: So he was there for them at all times?

J: All times. And still is – because they still use his military benefits.

K: That's good. How did you guys meet?

J: I was attending SUNO. My brother, Carl, was in the Air Force. I was drinking a little Boone's Farm, and I asked him if he had any cute GI's hanging around.

K: What is that?

J: A cute GI? It's just a cute guy that was in the military. And my husband just happened to be his roommate. He put Willy on the phone, and we started talking and talking, and writing, and writing, and fell in love. About five months later, we got married. We had Christy and Shawn, and he adopted Ronnie.

K: Oh. How did you recover from the loss of your father and the loss of your husband?

J: Oooh. I'm still in recovery. You don't recover from things like that. You just don't. I mean, you go on. It gets better with time. But, you just don't recover. I had a 21-gun salute, with my husband, and of course with me being a disabled veteran, I would also get one when I die. [But] I'm gonna be cremated, because I would not put my kids through that. If you love me, you love me now. I want people to remember me how I am. Seeing them in the casket and stuff like that was traumatic.

My youngest son didn't go to his father's funeral. I asked him, "Shawn, do you want to go?" He said,

"No, because people gonna be crying." So I knew he had a good reason, and he didn't want to deal with it. I don't want nothing negative or anything sticking in their minds about it.

K: So what made you come up with Kangaroo Court?

J: (Laughs) You have the best questions! We were in the military. I was an emergency room specialist. A nurse—I taught GI's under me how to suture. A lot of my records I can't tell you about, because they're still sensitive and classified. And I'm trying to declassify them now, because I'm muzzled.

But anyway, we were stationed there, and I had a slumber party for Krissy. There was about six of them there, and I was lying on the sofa. I woke to them arguing about something. And I said, "What's going on?" And one said this, and one said that. I was raised on Perry Mason, so I said, "Wait, wait, wait. We're just gonna play court." I was the judge and we settled it. Then they said they wanted to play again. And I said, "Wait, play again?! This is not a game. This is real stuff!" And they said, "No, we wanna play!"

One said, "I wanna be the judge this time! I wanna be this this time!" I was like, "Oh my goodness, what did I do?" I just took the paper and I tore them up, and I put them in a hat, and whoever pulled whatever, that's who they were. As we traveled around the world, and Krissy was at a slumber party, she said, "Mom, it's slow over here, why don't you come and play the court game?" After my husband died, we were living at 1740 Piety Street. I was in a deep depression then. My oldest son Ronnie might have been fourteen. He told me to do something with the game and see what happens.

I invented it for family and friends. I didn't want any of my family and friends to ever work [too hard], or ever worry about anything in life.

K: How do you think everything is coming along?

J: Perfectly. I was frustrated. I would give up. I would say, "How is this gonna work?" But you know, it had to work in God's time. He gave me the vision, and I saw it, but I would get sick because I have a bad heart   I have to have heart surgery, and I have fluid on the brain. I would get sick, and I would have to take my medicine. The kids would be at the different schools waiting for me to show up, and when I didn't make it there, it's like I'm lying to them.

The Christmas that just passed, when it snowed, I almost died at the VA hospital. That's the same hospital where my father died when I was twelve. They overdosed me on the wrong medication. I came

Jan with board members for Kangaroo Court

home Christmas Eve. I couldn't walk, I couldn't talk. I was going into renal failure. But every time I go in there and get sick, I come back out even stronger with the business.

K: Wow. So how did you feel about how they overdosed you with the wrong medicine?

J: I know the doctor accidentally did it, and I don't want to hurt his career, because I know it was purely an accident. But I want them to pay me for my disability. I'm forty percent disabled. But they really owe me one hundred percent disability—and that's what I'm fighting em for. For my heart. I had to fight them to right below the Supreme Court, and I won that one. If I die fighting them, Ronnie's gonna take it up, because I don't know how much damage that overdose did to my heart. The doctors at the hospital are really upset about it because they say the pharmacy should have caught it. I think everything happens for a reason. I'm still here. They have beautiful nurses up there that took care of me; during that time they were singing the Christmas Carols.

My boyfriend Henry [taught] me how to walk all over again. We met when I was twelve and he was eleven. He had just moved down there and he was my first crush. He was younger than me. In those days, you can't date anybody younger than you. We just had puppy love. This is our third time dating. The [second time] I had children then, so we couldn't really see each other the right way. I had to raise them.

INTERVIEW WITH MS. CECILE PAYNE

Ms. Cecile has taken over the Palm Tavern, a barroom on the corner of Clouet and Law, because her sister Mildred died. Before it was handed to Mildred, the bar was their father's and before him, it was his father's. So this bar is not just a hang out place, it's part of a tradition in their family. Everyone in the neighborhood calls it "Walter's."

My grandma and grandpa have always hung out there since I was small. I've known Ms. Mildred since I was little, too. She was in love with me. Every time I saw her, she gave me money. As a child I always wondered why she liked me so much. Every time we had parties she would always be there. She gave me a hug and a little bit of money. She always had that big smile with a cigarette and a drink, dancing to the music. After awhile, I stopped seeing her. I didn't know what to think until my grandma told me that she died of diabetes.

Ms. Cecile is very nice, just like her sister Mildred. I didn't know what she'd think if I came to interview her. When I did ask her, she was happy to do it and that made me feel more comfortable. When I got there, she waiting for me. I was surprised she was ready for the questions to be asked. She wanted to get the interview out of the way because a lot of her regular customers come in the morning. She invited me into a small room a couple of stairs higher from where the bar was. It had two tables and a few chairs with posters up of models with beers in their hand. She said she didn't want to talk about her sister because they were very close, and it still made her upset to think about her not being here anymore.

Kesha: Ms. Cecile, where did you grow up?

Cecile: I grew right down the street from this bar.

K: What was it like there?

C: To me, the neighborhood was, and is, beautiful. Some people call it a ghetto, but a ghetto to me is in the mind. We were just a bunch of hardworking people, and it was nice.

K: Can you describe it for someone who has never been there before?

C: There were more families. Husbands and wives with children. People liked to plant gardens. We grew tomatoes and lettuce. We had chickens in our yard.

The grown-ups community parented. Every parent took part with us. We had a large family. It was twelve of us. We all played together, worked together. It was very neighborly; everybody knew everybody. I had very loving parents: parents who believed in education and discipline, parents who encouraged us to believe in ourselves and know that we can accomplish anything that we put our minds to.

K: What did your parents do for a living?

C: My grandfather and father owned this bar. My mother was a homemaker.

K: What was your mom like?

C: My mom's name was Dorothy. She was sweet. With breakfast in the morning, dinner in the afternoon. We had to go to church.

K: What was your dad like?

C: My dad's name was Walter. He was a provider. We lived very well. We ate well, dressed well, and participated in different activities. He encouraged us not to get into the bar business, but to go on to college and pursue other things.

Thursday was the only day my father was off, so that was family day for us. In the summer he would always take us to Ponchartrain Lake to swim. Every-body in the neighborhood would jump in the back of the truck, and we would all go. Or they boiled crabs and crawfish in our backyard, and we would sit on the back steps and wait for everything to get done. We had a yard full of friends because everybody`wanted to come over.

K: What were the expectations people placed on women when you grew up?

C: I think, to go to school. The older women encouraged us to get an education, and not to depend on husbands because during mother's generation, lots of women didn't work out the home. And they did not want their daughters to be uneducated or not able to provide for themselves.

K: Did you agree with that?

C: At that time I didn't understand it, because I thought their life was great. You know, she didn't work. But now I do understand that women need to be independent, well educated, confident in themselves, trusting in God, and the rest will follow.

R: Did you ever spend time at the bar itself when you were little?

C: Oh no, we just came to the window, and he gave us free candy.

K: What role does the barroom serve in the neighborhood?

C: They employ people. We buy a lot of products, from paper towels, dishcloths, alcohol, cigarettes, you would be surprised at the number of vendors who profit from this business.

It's also a neighborhood spot that's been here over fifty years. Kesha's grandfather and great grandfather came here. Everybody in the neighborhood: great grandfathers, grandmothers, uncles, aunts were here. The children remember coming to that window because my father loved children, and we basically give candy away. I mean, we sell it for little or nothing, because it was for the children.

K: What are some of your favorite memories of the barroom?

C: A lot of food. A *lot* of food.

K: Did you ever think you would be running the bar?

C: Never. I never would have thought that this would be what I was doing. Never. The girls were discouraged from the bar business. I think because it was a worldly thing. It's partying, drinking and other things, and he didn't want that for us. I had three brothers, and they were being groomed. But

one brother went to the military, got married and moved to California. Another brother became ill young, and then the other brother just didn't want to do it. Mildred always worked here. She started working at the bar when she was seventeen, and so she just stayed.

K: What was your sister Mildred like?

C: She was cool. She was a party person. She was sort of bossy. She was very independent. No one could tell her what to do or what not to do. She ran the bar very firm, like my father and my grandfather did.

K: What are some of the differences in the way that your father, you, and your sister ran the bar?

C: We run it the same. My grandfather passed the rules and the regulations and the style to my father. My father passed it to my sister, my sister passed it on to me. I'm in the process of passing it on to my nephew.

We operate like a lounge, like if you would go to the Hilton lounge or any place else. People cannot come in here cursing, being disrespectful towards women, or towards each other. They can drink, party, laugh, but they cannot violate order. That's why we have been here more than fifty years. That's our basic foundation. You have to come in here and behave yourself. If someone gets drunk, usually that's not a big problem because their friends will tell them. They know they will be put out of this bar if they violate the rules. We respect each other and have fun. And that's what its about. It's not about a lot of drama. It's a place where we want men to bring their wives, and bring their daughters when they graduate. It's that type of atmosphere.

When they cross the door, most of the young men feel like they have arrived. "At last! I can come in!" A lot of the girls feel the same way. "I'm old enough now to come in!" They take a lot of pride in the fact that they cannot come in if you're a youngster. We do not allow youngsters in. They have to be represented by an older person if they are under thirty. Like Kesha: at a certain age, she can come in but she must come in with her grandfather or grandmother. She cannot just walk in. When they are represented, they take ownership in the club like their grandparents do.

K: How would you describe the regulars?

C: They are the nicest people in the world. They are all employed. They are the cement finishers, your truck drivers, your teachers, your custodians. They come from all walks of life. This is home base for them. We have hundreds and hundreds and hundreds of people who come through here because we've been here so long. They come from Slidell, Covington, Metairie, Kenner. All over the place.

We do a lot of eating. We have seafood on Tuesday, fish plates on Sunday. Every other day we have all kinds of snacks. We have the Blue Monday beans, so we keep that [tradition] going.

K: How would you describe the Ninth Ward for someone who hasn't been there before?

C: I think it's a mixed bag. I think there are a lot of good families— hard-working families— with good values. And we also have those people who have fallen in the cracks for whatever the reason. I think that the people in the Ninth Ward need to be more aggressive in keeping their neighborhoods free of drugs and all the other problems. I think that they depend on someone else, when they need to realize it's us. We don't have trouble on this corner. We don't allow none of that.

R: And how do you keep the younger guys off your corner?

C: Reputation. They know they're not wanted. If too many of them even come close, we call the fifth district. The Fifth District [Police Station] cooperates with us. They'll drive by and they'll scatter. But most of them know: You're not welcome, and you will not be allowed to stay here.

K: What do you do in your free time?

C: Since I've been running the bar, I don't have much time, but I did manage to plant some tomatoes. But it's busy all the time.

R: What were you doing before here?

L: I was retired. I was at home resting. Not even thinking about working!

K: What have you been most happy about in your life so far?

L: Uh, I think to have reached a point in life where I'm financially secure. I've made wise investments and saved. I think I'm most proud about that.

K: If you had to do some things over again, what would they be?

L: I think I would not have returned to New Orleans, because I find that it's an up and down economic thing for black people. I don't think it's a good place for African-Americans to live. I've lived in Denver, Nebraska, and Kansas City. I think there are more opportunities in other places. I think that all young African-Americans should leave.

K: Thank-you.

REGULARS TALK ABOUT WALTER'S

Issac Boyle and Ralph Howard

Question: How long have you been coming here?

Ralph Howard: Oh, shucks. Since the sixties. Some of my friends used to hang here before that. I'm a retired steam plant engineer.

Q: And what is that?

R: I work at the water board. We put turbines in, service turbines, control the water pressure for the city.

Q: How would you describe it for someone who's never been here before?

R: It's just a place that a lot of regulars come in the morning. It's a fun place. Most people here are nice people. That's the best way I can describe it.

Q: How long have you been coming to the bar?

Issac Boyle: That's a good question. About forty years.

Q: And what was it like when you first came here?

I: I heard about it. My father used to be here all the time. This has always been a nice place. Everybody who comes in feels very comfortable, and they come back. People all over the city come in. That's the most important thing. All the years I've known it we've never had anything bad happen, and I'm here kind of regular.

They have order in here. You don't do everything you wanna do. You do things according to order, the rules. Any place where there's no rules, there's no business.

Q: What are the rules?

I: No loud cursing and hollering, no downing other people, and things like that. We don't have the youngsters in here, cuz when we was young ourselves, it was a different class of people than it is today. That's what makes this place special. That's why people come here. You can bring your wife, your girlfriend, your sweetheart, or whoever here - and it's no problem because they'll be respected. That's why.

Most people who come here today, their grandfather, their grandparents, they was in this place.

R: My kids come in sometimes, but they're all grown, in their thirties.

Q: Is this known as, "My dad's place to hang out."

R: Yep, yep. They'll call and say, "Is my dad home?"

Q: And, are you retired? Or are you still working?

I: No, I'm retired.

Q: And what were you doing when you were working?

I: I was a longshoreman. A longshoreman superintendent.

Q: So you've been all over the world.

I: Quite a few places. I've been all overseas and everything.

Q: And what makes the Ninth Ward a special place?

I: Well, there's no place like home.

Q: Like I said a little while ago, you feel comfortable in here.

I: Very comfortable. Anywhere you go you'll always have a place to come back to and call it home. That's what makes it special.

Q: What kind of music is played?

I: A variety of music.

Q: What are the favorite songs that people play?

R: Adult type music, you know. Very little hip hop—we don't have that. And no rap. I can't stand that music. I like the old blues. We have BB King.

I: We got a variety over here.

Cecile: Usher –

Q: Usher goes, but no rap.

I: No rap.

Kesha: I like it.

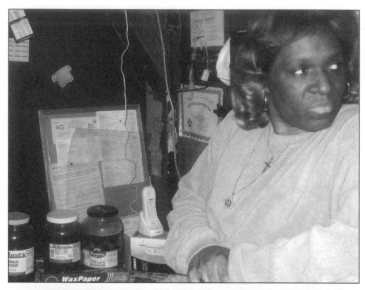

Vanessa Thomas. Occupation: Bartender. "I've been working at the bar for four years. It's family. The customers have been coming here for forty years. They even cater to children. It's the only bar that I know of that does that. A lot of kids that came to that window are grown now. It's unique."

Curtis Price, Jr.: Occupation: Retired from 33 years at Boh Brothers Construction.

 I used to sneak in when I was too young. My daddy and his friends used to come in. I'd want a dollar or something and ask, "Is my daddy in here?" They'd yell at me, "Get away from here—you're too young."

The drugs and the youngsters don't come in here. You don't have to worry about the crime. They need more places like this to save the city. It was beautiful at one time. People are scared of their own children these days. This is what we got left. We got to deal with it.

Jorge Philip. Place of Birth: Honduras. Mr. Walter used to cash checks for us.

The Kool-Aid Kid. Occupation: Truck Driver. I've been coming here since my father was living.

Willie Thomas and Michael Armstrong

Calvin Martin: Occupation: Self-employed mechanic.

My mom and dad stay down the street. I grew up down this way and I'm gonna stay down here until I die. A lot of them get a few dollars and move out to the East. Not me. I'm comfortable.

I've been coming since I was eighteen. I like the peace and quiet. No youngsters. No humbug. It looks like I'm the youngest one in here and I'm forty-four years old. "

INTERVIEW WITH MS. IONA BOSEMAN

There are so many churches in the Ninth Ward. You see them on every corner you turn. Some are big brick buildings while others are made out of houses with a small steeple and a few stained glass windows. On Sundays, everything's quiet. Nobody's outside except between eleven and three o'clock when church is getting out. Most of the churches are "come as you are" and wear regular clothes, but in others, people dress up. They wear pants or skirt suits, with big matching hats decorated with pearls or ribbon. The colors this season are red, pink, white, and black. The men wear casual shirts, slacks, and shiny leather shoes. People linger outside talking about what they're going home to eat. Most women prepare food on Saturdays so they can come back from church and just warm it up.

I go to Greater St. Stephen Missionary Baptist Church in New Orleans East. It is a very big church with three locations. A lot of people say that my church is about money because they have an ATM machine in it. But if you look at it, you might need some quick money, and there's an ATM to solve that.

My church has at least seventy benches. There is upstairs and a crying room for the babies and for the people who catch the Holy Ghost very often. The choir stands in one big spot close to Bishop Martin. When he preaches, he breaks it down in so many

ways you wouldn't even think of. He'll make you feel and see things from different angles to where you can take it all up in your hands. You'll just feel so good that you cry and jump all around because you've found a breakthrough.

Growing up I was told it was important to go to church so that I could learn more about the Lord and life. I just try to do the right thing so that I can go to Heaven when my journey is over. But people don't necessarily have to go to church because they can watch it on TV or go about it by the Bible. One thing I'd never heard of before was running a church out of a house. A regular house that you wake up to every morning— one where you clean up, cook and wash, and do other house things when it's not used for worship. As I was writing my book, though, I found out that my neighbor Ms. Iona Boseman ran a small church out of her house for many years.

I asked her if she would do an interview for my book, and she invited me over one afternoon and showed me where she has held services for many years. It was in a small back room of her house. She had fold- up chairs instead of benches, an organ and a small pulpit. Throughout her house, there were pictures of her family members and religious prints of scenes from the Bible. In the interview I found out about her life and how the church began.

Kesha: Ms. Iona, where did you grow up?

Iona: I grew up on the Uptown area. 2710 Josephine Street. I lived up there for about 18 years.

K: What was it like there?

I: Oh, it was just a real neighborhood. We didn't have fans, or air conditioning, or anything, so we would sit outside at night until about 12 o'clock in the summertime. The block was full of children and we would play with them until after a while, everybody come and sit on the steps.

We didn't have a television or radio. At one time, we didn't have electricity. The older people would scare us by telling us about the devil man. They said you could be walking along, and all of a sudden this person could just appear right beside you. Naturally, you didn't want to go inside. The windows would be open and the only thing you could think about was, "Hey, that devil man is gonna come."

We used to just sit around and tell stories. Some you would hear over and over, but you would still be afraid. You sit there, and they'd be telling, "Mary, I'm in your back room. Mary, I'm in your front room." And then all the sudden they would say, "Mary—I GOT YOU!"

K: I remember that game. Can you describe your family?

I: Well, I am the second of nine. My mother had five girls and four boys. The neighborhood was family-oriented. We were poor, but nobody knew that we were poor because everybody was poor. That's the way it was.

We had a fireplace in the third room of our house, and that's where we all sat around in the winter. We'd start the fire off with wood, but then we used to burn stone coal. It's black, and it's hard. We had four rooms and a bathroom: a living room, where my dad and mother slept on the sofa, and then we had two more rooms and the kitchen.

My mother was a good cook. We ate a lot of beans. We had beans every day for dinner, but not on Sundays. Sunday was the big day: stewed chicken and rice and gravy, macaroni and cheese, green peas, and potato salad. My mother had a big pan, and we had peach cobbler.

We would go to Sunday school at nine-thirty. Our church was First Evangelist Baptist Church. We would run to Sunday school when the last bell rang and then we stayed for the 11 o'clock service. Afterwards, we went home and ate.

While we were eating dinner, sometimes we would hear the band. Everybody would jump up, leave the food on the table, run to the corner of Magnolia to watch the parade go by. A lot of people would be second lining, but we knew we'd better not go any further than that. My mother and dad weren't into nothing like that. Afterwards, we would come back and eat.

We washed the dishes and, then we went back to church for Baptist Training Union. And we stayed for night church. Would you have liked to stay in church like that?

And then for Carnival, we did a lot of walking and everything passed right on the corner from us, too. They had a lot of Indians, but that's something I've always been afraid of. The Indians and those Zulus. I look at it but I don't get close to it. At one time they used to fight, but now they fight with the dress. At one time, they would carry knives and guns. When the tribes would meet up together, they were really frightening. I guess that's why I was afraid of them. Then, a lot of people in the country would mask, too. Sometimes this was the way people would get back at each other. If you're masked, a lot of times they didn't know who they were.

K: Where were your parents from?

I: My mother is from White Castle. My dad was from Donaldsonville, which is ten miles apart. My mother worked at a plantation, cutting sugar cane. They tell me a relative of ours still works there as a guide.

I was born in White Castle. I'm the only one out of the nine that was born there. My older sister was born here. My mother couldn't go to the hospital, but she had a doctor from Touro that came to her. My grandmother would always send someone here to be with her when she was pregnant, but she couldn't find anybody when I was born, so my mother was in the country. That's why I was born in the country.

I was the only one who didn't like the country. My sisters and brothers would go out there in the summer— not me. It was very, very dark. There was a highway at one end, and the levee at the other end.

K: What did your family do for a living?

I: First, my dad worked at the Leidenheimer's bakery shop. The bakery shop is still there. You know, where they make the French bread? He worked there back in the thirties. My dad's salary was $18.75 a week, and they was trying to get an increase in salary to $25 dollars. The boss said he isn't gonna pay it, so the union comes in. It's an organization that comes in to help give you better working conditions. My dad went out with them, even though the boss and him got along very well together. He thought my dad wouldn't go out on strike, but my dad wouldn't cross the picket line. Everybody would stop working and go out picketing, so that would stop the job from moving. I think my dad was the only one they didn't hire back. My dad did a little gardening work until he joined the union as a longshoreman.

K: Why did you decide to move to the Ninth Ward after you had your home base in Uptown so long?

I: Well, the lady bought the house. It was a double house, and like I say, we had a fireplace, and it was cold. You see, we used to have the four seasons. It would be a distinct difference and in the winter, it used to be cold here. She moved on one side, and she put gas on her side, but she wouldn't put gas on the other side while going up on the rent. So we just went on and moved.

That's why we came down. It was kind of strange when we first came down here, because it seemed like it was so far from everything. We were used to being Uptown where everything was right in the neighborhood, close. And we knew everybody that was Uptown.

I: We moved down here in 1954. This whole neighborhood was white. This street was not paved—it was just dirt. We moved to this house right after Hurricane Betsy in 1965.

K: How would you describe the Ninth Ward for someone who's never been here?

I: It's okay for me, but it's quieter than it was uptown. We had more going on Uptown. But then it could be because I was younger that I was, you know, experiencing this. I don't think I would like to live Uptown again. I don't think I'd like to live there again.

CHURCH

K: How did you begin your church?

I: When we moved down here, we were looking for a place to continue going to Sunday school. My children were small then, and I was looking cuz that was so far to go Uptown. My little sister was an organist over here at St. Luke. She started taking the children, and I said, "Well look, I think we'll go to Sunday school over there." The superintendent was Brother Rachel. He was an old man. He just died about two years ago at 95 years old. He was a former Catholic and very informed on that Bible.

He didn't get along so well with the minister, so he decided he was going to leave the church. I said, "Brother Rachel, why don't we have service at my house?" He said, "Oh, Sister Russell, that would be nice." We started here in 1986 and we've been here ever since. Right now, we're over at my sister's house because my brother-in-law is sick, and he can't walk, so we're having it over at his house on Louisa Street. At one time, we had a good bit of members. We had a youth group, but the children grew up. Some went

to the service, some went to college and some people have died out. But we have a good little group.

K: So are you the minister here?

I: No, I'm not a minister, babe. My son-in-law is the superintendent now.

K: So how would you describe the congregation?

I: My church? Mostly family. And everybody gets along well. Most of us are Baptist, but we have had some Catholics come. My son-in-law is a former

Catholic. His mother used to come, but she fell and she broke her hip. We have Methodist people come. It's just like a soup. Like a gumbo.

K: How do you get your members?

I: Whoever wants to come, can come. I've been trying to get a lot of people around here to come — the man next door used to tell me, "Oh, Ms. Russell, I'm coming over, I'm coming over." I invite a lot of people—this is what you're supposed to do. I try to get to reach some of the little fellas that be hanging around: "Why don't you come to church?" "Oh, Ms. Russell, I'm coming, I'm coming!" But sometimes they never do. All you can do is tell them.

K: What goals do you have for the church?

I: The goal that we have for the church is just to serve others, to help bring people in to know the word of God. That's what we do. We give our money — because we are tithers —to different churches and different organizations. I went to Union Baptist Seminary and I made a donation to them for about $10,000 dollars. Brother Rachel made a donation of $20,000 to his former Catholic Church out in Natchitoches.

We just blessed a church where my son plays. He drives an 18-wheeler but he's home on the weekends

on Franklin. We all are ambassadors, it's not just the preacher. Whoever I see, I'm supposed to tell you about God.

K: How does the church help people recover from loss?

I: When somebody's sick, we try to help. Like my brother-in-law right now. My sister had to pay three hundred dollars for some medicine, so we gave the money to him for medicine. We help the members when they are in distress. And we help the youngsters that have graduated from here, too.

K: What do you do in your free time, besides church?

I: I volunteer for Charity Hospital on Mondays in their Volunteer Office. And I keep time and things for the Council of the Aging. I don't belong to that, but I just help the lady that's head of that there.

When I first retired, I went to Union Seminary for four years. And then I went to school for drawing for two years. I decided I had finished what I wanted to do, so I thought, "I think I'll give some time to Charity." Charity and Universal work together now. A lot of things go through Charity Hospital. They even have people that get free medicine through there.

Four of my children were born there. My youngest brother was a mason, and he went by my son's house after a meeting. He said he didn't feel good. It was about one o'clock in the morning. Andy was driving him to the hospital, and he wanted to go to Veterans, but Andy said he didn't know how to get into Veterans, so he just drove him right to Charity Hospital. My brother grabbed his heart like this and said, "OH!" Andy drove him with one hand on the wheel and one hand holding his head up. They got into Charity Hospital, and the guard just grabbed him up and brought him in. He had an aneurysm, and they saved his life.

K: What have you been most happy about in your life so far?

I: Well, I'm happy, first, that I have God in my life. I know Him. And I know, when I leave here, where I'm going. That's the main thing. I've tried to stress that to everybody all the time: the only thing that's going to be important to you when you come to the end of your journey will be God. And I'm happy that I have children—they're pretty good children, and I've had a pretty good life.

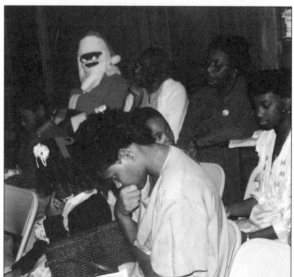

INTERVIEW WITH EVELLA "MS. COOCHIE" PIERRE

I met Ms. Coochie when she moved to North Miro from the Desire Projects. She's a very straightforward person and tells very interesting stories. Throughout her life, she has been very active in social and pleasure clubs' second line parades. A number of years ago, she helped her son Louis begin one of the most important clubs to come out of the Ninth Ward: the Nine Times Social and Pleasure Club.

GROWING UP IN THE 7TH WARD

I grew up in the Seventh Ward on North Miro and Pauger. That's where I was born and raised. My mama did the nursery work and my daddy was a seaman, a merchant marine.

My daddy gave me the name Coochie. When he was staying in Germany, and he would ask, "How is my Coochie Coo?" And he kept on calling me that. I like that name more than I like my real name. My children always tell me, "Ma, that's not your name. Your name is Evella." But when someone asks, I say, "Coochie."

The Seventh Ward was all about Indians. We come up around all that. I had a lot of people in my family that masked. I had a cousin named Patsy, who used to mask as an Indian from a child until she got grown. We knew just about all of them that were masking. We were like family. So we knew they were masking, and would go around their house when they would come out of their house.

Mardi Gras Day was the Indian's day. They could hold up an eighteen-wheeler if it's coming down the street. When they put them suits on, they got a whole different personality. They really change their attitude once they put their suits on. They don't want to talk to nobody, they don't want nobody to touch them, they don't want nobody to hug them and kiss them. They don't want nobody to get close to their suits. You can sit there and help them sew their suits or their patches, but once they put their suits on, their whole attitude changes. To me it's like they got crazy to me. They be stone crazy.

The Wildman would come, and he truly came wild. He'd have real bones. They aren't gonna ask you to move. They gonna be all on top of you. The best thing your mama told you was, "Stay inside, don't go out there; wait til they pass." You got to peep out the door or look out the window.

We were with our mama on Mardi Gras Day. We would leave our house and walk to Claiborne before they put the interstate up there, and find a spot. We'd put our blanket down, and that's where we would stay. My mama was scared to death of skeletons. I could remember we were around Claiborne and Orleans. My sister Jacquelyn was a baby. My mama hit a skeleton over the head and broke the baby's bottle over the man's head.

SECOND LINES

When my mama said, "We're going to a second line, get ready," we put our regular little clothes on and our tennies, and we'd be gone. My mother's brothers and her nephew were members of The Jolly Bunch. It was a traditional club. They didn't dress in suits. They wore a pair of slacks, suspenders, a shirt, and a hat. They had baskets that they would decorate. They would ride on cars. And that was what second lines were all about then. The band that everybody would really get was the Olympia Brass Band.

I can remember my mama and them used to go to the florist to get baskets and if they didn't have them there, then they'd go to the Holt Graveyard and get baskets off people's graves. Back then, people used to put flowers in big baskets on the graves. They was out there robbing the dead. They'd come home and decorate them with flowers. Some of them had little baby dolls in their basket. But it wasn't nothing that they would give out to nobody.

At the parades, all six of us children would be right behind our mama—holding on to each other. We had a bag with all our little sandwiches for us to eat. If you got thirsty, that was your business. Maybe she liked them so much because she came up around them.

I guess it just was in her blood because everybody in my family loves second lines. I would miss eight hours of work to go to a second line. I was working at the Marie Antoinette hotel at Toulouse and Dauphine, and if they had a jazz funeral in the Sixth Ward, we would ask our boss could we go. And my boss knew to give me Sunday off. If she didn't give it then I was going to take it off. Every Sunday, "Evella, do they have a second line? Okay, Evella's off." Everybody knew I was gonna take off to go to a second line.

DESIRE

My mama moved to Desire in 1956. I didn't want to be in the project, period, that's why I stayed with my grandmother. I stayed more with my grandmother than I did my mama. The only time you didn't see me with her was when she was going to work. But other than that, you saw both of us together, walking down the street, holding hands.

When I lived across the Canal with her, Sundays were strictly church. I didn't really worry about going to second lines. We would go to church seven days a week and twice on a Sunday. That's right, I was a church-going girl. When Hurricane Betsy came through here, we moved in with my mama because our house was under water. But after the water went down, they cleaned everything up, and we moved back in our house.

I think that I was sixteen years old when I really started to stay by my mama. I was going to Carver school then. I quit school in tenth grade. Instead of going to school, I was gonna look for me a job. I think if I would have stayed with my grandmother, I wouldn't have gotten pregnant at sixteen—my grandma wouldn't play that. I was married when I was seventeen. I was with [my husband] seven years. And he went into the service, and it was just a conflict with his mama and me and my baby. I let all of that go. I didn't want to be married back then anyway. But back then, two parents would just sit down and plan a wedding. As far as I was concerned, he could just be my baby's dad and leave me alone. I wanted my baby just to have his last name.

I've been divorced since 1969 or somewhere around there. And I haven't remarried yet. My husband's been married, I think, three times. He's the pastor of Living Witness up on Oretha Castle Haley Boulevard. I never worried about marrying nobody.

BLACK PANTHERS

The Black Panthers was an organization. Half of them was from right here in New Orleans. I had read about them in the paper, you know, but that's all. I was about twenty-nine when I heard that they were coming to Desire. Everybody wanted to be where they were.

People really thought the Black Panthers was a threat to the area, to the community, but they were not a threat. They were in the community to help

people. They'd feed the children breakfast, and after school they'd help them with their homework. My kids went to the breakfast programs. My mama didn't want them to go, though. She said, "Somebody's going to get hurt over there." I told her, "Well, you keep 'em, cuz I'm goin."

The Panthers had a house back there on Piety and Higgins. It's a [vacant] lot now. And they were all in there, and the police came and shot it up. And then they took an apartment over in the Desire. The police broke them up and they all went to jail for possession of fire arms and trespassing.

That day it was chaos. They had helicopters flying and shooting from the sky. They came back there with tanks. And everybody formed a circle around [the building] so that they wouldn't get to a door where they were. They [eventually] got busted by a mailman—a person pretending he was delivering mail. He was undercover. He was a police. And that's how they got into the apartment where he was.

RAISING CHILDREN

What was my address? 3702 Pleasure. Apartment B. When I was raising my children up back there in Desire, it was a whole lot better. We could go to bed without locking our doors at night. Sit outside all night long, drinking ice chests of beer. I would leave my door open and go to Louisa Street to the store. I come back home, and it would be just how I left my house. I never worried about nobody coming in my house. My thing was, "If a damn fool come in here, he must not know Coochie live here." But if they know I live there, they ain't coming in here.

I raised four girls and one boy. I never had no trouble out none of my children. I was that type of a mama: "If you wrong, you wrong." You know, don't come to me and tell me, "Ma, so and so." I don't want to hear about it. I want to hear what you did. I told them, "Trouble's easy to get into, but it's hard to get out." But I also taught them, "Don't let nobody mess over you. Don't let nobody do what they want to do to ya."

I was the type of a mama where if my children went somewhere, I would go bring them where they had to go and pick them up. I had a Maverick. I would have so many children in my car until they used to call my Maverick an 18-wheeler. I used to get so mad with them, I said, "The rest of these children ain't got no mama?"

My children was real close. Louis didn't hide nothing from the girls, and they didn't hide nothing from him. That was their only brother. They loved him. He knew everything about them. He knew when they turned young ladies and everything else. I was home from work and he said, "Ma."

"What?"

"Somebody became a young lady today."

Everything they had, they kept it among themselves. If they got too far out of proportion, then they would come to me, and I would tell em, "Well, y'all didn't tell me when it happened, I don't want to know nothing about it. Y'all sort it out." If he got into something with somebody at the barroom Magee's, he'd call my oldest daughter "I got into it with so and so, I don't carry no gun, I don't carry no knife. Come get me." And she gonna get her brother.

LOUIS

Louis was a person that believed in making peace with you. If y'all are friends, and he see that y'all arguing and fighting, he's gonna tell y'all, "Y'all friends. Why y'all want to fight one another?" If he had a dollar and you needed fifty cents, he's gonna give you that fifty cents, and he gonna keep fifty cents. One time he was in half of a body cast. He got hurt playing football. I used to go into the bath-

room and bathe him. He was a teenager. They say, "Man, you let your mama was you?" He said, "That's all who's gonna wash me. My mama."

I used to go to Indian practice at the Caldonia and Mama Ruth's barroom [that's now Joe's Cozy Corner]. When he was seventeen he said, "Ma, you know all the Indians. You know all the songs. When I get eighteen, I'm going with you." I said, "No, you're not coming with me. You're going to go in the barroom by your own self, because I don't hang in the barroom with my children. I'll hang in the barroom with anybody else's children, but not mine."

He went anywhere he wanted to go from one end of New Orleans to the other end, and nothing ever happened to him. I never thought nobody back there would take his life. He died August 6, 2000. All I know is "attempted robbery." And he didn't have money on him. And so I don't know what the hell they wanted. It was on Higgins and Louisa, right there by the bus stop.

When he got killed, nobody came to tell me. They went to my sister's house and told her. He loved my sister Glenda, baby. He really thought that was his mama for real. And he used to tell me when he was small, "You're not my mama. You're too black. Glenda my mama." She was red and so was he until he started working for Boh Brothers Construction Company and then he started getting darker by working in the sun. My daughters had left out my house. They were going to see if it was really true before they came and tell me. They were that close.

I remember the year before he got killed, we got him a band for his birthday by Magee's. That boy was so drunk that he couldn't stand up on his own. I told him, "You know what? This is the last damn band I'm gonna get you. The next band I'm gonna get for you is when you die." But when he got killed, the Nine Times Club got the band for him. He had a horse-drawn carriage.

He was at Spirit of Sunlight on Independence and Rocheblave. They left from the church, and they cut his body loose at Louisa and Higgins. Everybody was saying, Louis was the first person that came out of Desire to come through there with a horse-drawn jazz funeral.

CARE TAKING

I took care of my mama for ten years until she died. And she died here, in this house. I took care of that old lady for ten years! Got beat up by her and everything. Her pastor called her Muhammad Ali.

At the beginning, I could tell something was wrong with my mama. She was a missionary at church and I was the only one of her girls that could iron her uniform. Every week, this was my routine. She had four white uniforms and the cap.

She had enough to last her from one Sunday to the next. I would iron all of them and bring them to her house. [One day] I came over and I said, "Mom, why your table all full of this and that?"

"Oh, I don't know. I waste that coffee, I waste that sugar." Now, I was going to wipe it up, and it was dried on the table. And one day I went back there and I saw her telephone bill. I said, "You know they're about to disconnect your lights and your phone?" I knew something there was wrong with her.

I'll never forget when my mama went to the hospital. My children were on their way to church and I was on my way to the second line. My daughter calls and says "Ma, Maw Maw don't look right." Usually, before they get in the car, Maw Maw will hit them. But this time Maw Maw didn't tell them nothing.

I said, "Well. just take her straight to the hospital and I'll meet you with her medication and stuff." And when my daughter got to the hospital, they told the people she was having a stroke. That was when they diagnosed her with the early stage of Alzheimer's.

The first thing that came out the doctor's mouth was, "Put her in a home." My mama had too many daughters to be put in a home. I had a room that was a room for my grandchildren, so they lost their room because I gave that room to my mama. I'm going to deal with my momma the way I wanna deal with her.

When she first was diagnosed with Alzheimer's, I let her do for herself. "Ma, you gonna fix us some breakfast this morning?"

"I don't know."

I say, "Yeah, go fix me a sunny-side up egg. Go fix me two of them eggs." I would wash her clothes and bring them to her. "I don't know how to fold em up." I said, "Well, roll em up, do whatever. Just put them in your drawer cuz that's your clothes and I'm not going to fold them." I don't wait on her hand and foot. They told me when you do that, that make them go down faster.

We were staying in the projects then, and I had like a double lock on my door, because several times she had walked away, and we couldn't find her. But it would always happen that somebody know her and would see her. They had to get beat up, but they would always bring her back.

When she got in her second stage of Alzheimer's, there was a lot of things that she couldn't do no more. And when she got to be full blown Alzheimer's, well, she just couldn't do nothing. When she got full blown Alzheimer's, that lady wasn't nothing nice to put up with.

It was a full time job. Home Help would come every day of the week and bathe her. Bring her diapers and pads and stuff like that. I got her bed through the Home Help. I got her wheelchair through Home Help. I got her walker. Just about everything she had I got it through the government.

STRESS

I have an article that I cut out the paper, it was "The Caretaker That Forgot to Take Care of Themselves." When I read that in the paper, I said, "That's me." You know. I was going to the doctor because I always did suffer with my pressure, but that's all— I wasn't really taking care of myself. I was making sure my mama was comfortable, and she had everything that she needed, because I wasn't going to neglect her.

I had my first heart attack in 2000. The doctor said it was a lot of stress I was under. And my children told him, "Well, my brother got killed, and my mama takes care of her mama. And my Maw Maw has Alzheimer's." The doctor said I've held a lot of things in me from when my son got killed and also from dealing with my mama. Then I had another one about three years ago. They had to do the open-heart surgery with that one.

Like I tell everybody, I think when I had this open-heart surgery, my mother really started giving up. She saw I wasn't coming in her room. You know, it was my daughter and them coming to do for her now. Not me. I couldn't lift her up any more, you know. And after that, she really gave up. One day, they were talking about how I had the heart attack. She said, "Coochie? When you had a heart attack?' I said, "You remember when I wasn't in this house for a month?"

She said, '"No."

I said, "Well, I wasn't in here with you for a whole month. I was in the hospital."

And she said, "Lord, have mercy. My child had a heart attack? I'm gonna pray for you." And I said, "OK, Ma, that's what you do, you pray for me."

The same day that my mama passed, she said to my little grandson, "Hey little boy. Little boy. Get that ball. And let's play pitch and catch with the ball." They said she played with him up in here. That evening, when it was time for my daughter to come wash and get her ready for bed. I looked at her, and I said to myself, "My mama is leaving here." I went in her closet and chose a little shift dress that clamp down the front I said, "When you wash Mama, put that on her." She was dying then.

She died around 5:30 p.m. and she stayed right there in her bed until almost nine o'clock at night. Everybody was in that room, just like she was lying in her bed. My auntie was sitting in her little spot where she sat every time she came in. They were sitting there talking about church and praying.

N. MIRO

The Desire being torn down was like a heartache to me, but the Lord opened up a door for me to get out of the project, and as long as I can afford to stay out here, I'm going to stay. When I moved out, I signed my papers stating that I didn't want to return. There was too much memories of my son back there. I kept up with people I like. Some of them, I don't care to be talking to.

I'm used to being in an area where you see your neighbors. Around here, you don't see anybody. I'm more of an outside person than I am an inside person. And I'm not used to staying inside. I'm not used to keeping my door locked. Every time someone comes, I have to get up and open up the door.

And see, my children are always telling me, "Ma, you be bored around here, cuz they don't have nothing for you to do." There's nobody's business for me to get in around here. I think I sit outside more than anybody around here. When it's summertime, you might pass around here and I'll be sittin on the porch until 2 o'clock in the morning.

THE STORY OF THE NINE TIMES SOCIAL & PLEASURE CLUB

Ms. Coochie has been involved in the Nine Times Social Club since the beginning because her son Louis was one of the founding members. Louis had been second lining since he was a little boy. When he got up in age, he wanted to lead his own. Ms. Coochie explains, "He always wanted to parade in a second line club. The first club I let him come out with was the Jolly Bunch when he was three or four years old because I had two uncles and a cousin that were original Jolly Boys."

Lady Nine Times president Charlena Mathews says second lining was a part of life for many families in Desire. "A lot of us got it from out parents; they used to do that anytime. They have this one man, Uncle Pick. He had a pick-up truck. On Sundays, he used to come in the back of Desire and he would pull up. Everybody would be like, 'You going to the second line? You going to the second line?' It was all ages. He would fill up the truck until there was no room for nobody else and drive us to the beginning of the second line. He'd drop us off and ride from stop to stop. It was every Sunday like clockwork! I used to be like, 'Look Mom, what do I gotta clean up and do?'"

Ms. Coochie remembers Louis feeling the same way.

"Every Sunday, Louis would get right on that truck and be gone. When he got older, he said he just wanted to get a club out of Desire. But I kept telling him it wasn't going to work out. When you say parade, you're talking about serious money. He was determined to get a club out of the projects. And he wound up really doing it."

Everybody that's in the social aid and pleasure club prepares for the anniversary parade all year. They have to plan out what to wear, what colors, who the band will be, and what the route is going to be. Charlena explains, "You know, with second lines they're looking at how you're dressed and what you're working with, and what you got in your hand, and who you got following you. Who your king and queen is and everything. All that plays a role in it."

There are many other people who support the club throughout the year and especially during the parades. Ms. Coochie has always been around to

help. Grand Marshall Jean Nelson says, "She has her door open for us every year."

When the Nine Times paraded for the first time, "They all cried," Ms. Coochie recalls, "because a lot of people said they wasn't going to make it. They weren't going to parade. But they did." In 2000, Louis was made king in honor of his work in getting a club started in Desire. "My children bought all the decorations. They went to church and then went to decorate the barroom. Raymond, Pat, and Parker's mamas and me cooked a breakfast for them at the community center."

The Nine Times is one of the first official second line clubs from the Ninth Ward that got off the ground. Charlena explains, "It's like a big step for the us because we never actually had it done downtown. They call down here country. When you go uptown, that's where it all go down. Nine Times put the Ninth Ward on the map when they parade. We made *The Louisiana Weekly* newspaper for having the largest crowd at a second line

COMING OUT THAT DOOR

There's always a large crowd gathered at the beginning of a second line parade. You can really get to see what a person can do by seeing them step out the door. In addition to the dancing, it's an amazing moment to be greeted by your family. Charlena says, "So many of your family members and other people come out to see you. My mama was very sick at the time, and she told me to go. My mother died August 28th, and we paraded that year on Thanksgiving. If she didn't tell me to go with them, I would never be coming out that door. And that's a blessin for me. It was good."

Jean agrees, "It's a beautiful feeling. You have to try it first in order to know. To get that rush coming out that door. It feels scary and everything when you look out there, and you see all the people. Girl, but once you get out there, you just go all out and do whatever you have to do. It just be beautiful,."

Charlena says The Nine Times second line is like a reunion for residents. "You get to see people you haven't seen in awhile. At second lines you get to say: 'Oh, girl, I haven't seen you in a long, long time.' 'How your mama and them?' And everybody greeting everybody. It's a tradition that's still going on, but a lot of people was afraid to come forward to it.

Today, they're not afraid, and they come out there. People come out there, and they dance and have a good time."

It's true. Jean says. "People who were down here when we first started parading make sure they come back every year."

NINE TIMES 2004

To honor her support of the social and pleasure-club, Ms. Coochie was made Queen of Nine Times for 2004. She decided to wear African attire because, "I'm not a gown person. I don't like all that. And I didn't want a crown on my head because of my age. Not that I was too old, but it wasn't my style. I liked the way I was dressed."

The entire neighborhood looks forward to the Nine Times parade coming by Ms. Coochie's house. By the time the parade arrived on North Miro, the street was packed with people. The band played, "I'll Fly Away" in honor of Louis, and people kept dancing in the street after they stopped in front of Ms. Coochie's house. Their feet never stopped.

Most of the people on the block love to see the second line stop on my block. They only get a view of it once a year. Even though most of the people on my block are old, they still know how to get down when the second line stops. Everybody who is usually inside comes out for Nine Times.

Mrs. Frey says, "They have so many people out there, and then they have a truck that cooks. Oh! We have so much fun. Some people stay by our house for a little while until the parade leaves again. Coochie and her family clean up after the parade."

"It is just fun. I don't know how to second line, but the music makes you wanna shake or whatever you want to do. At my age, I won't be doing nothing like that. But the second line, you would enjoy it."

THE NEIGHBORHOOD STORY PROJECT
OUR STORIES TOLD BY US

What you have just read is one of the five books to come from the first year of the Neighborhood Story Project. This has been an incredible year for us, and we thank you for your support and attention.

The Neighborhood Story Project would like to give a big shout out to the people of the City of New Orleans—y'all are the best. Thank you for showing so much love.

There are lots of folks and organizations that have made this possible. You have come through with stories, with food, with love, and with money—and believe us when we say that all four are necessary.

First off, we'd like to acknowledge our great partners, the Literacy Alliance of Greater New Orleans and the University of New Orleans. Specifically, Peg Reese, Rachel Nicolosi, Rick Barton, Tim Joder, Bob Cashner, Susan Krantz and Jeffrey Ehrenreich have been excellent supervisors and colleagues.

To Steve Gleason and Josselyn Miller at the One Sweet World Foundation. Thank-you for getting this project from the very beginning, and for having such awesome follow through.

To the institutions of the city that have been good to us—thank you. Good institutions play such an important role in making a place. Specifically we'd like to thank the Greater New Orleans Foundation, The Lupin Foundation, The Louisiana Endowment for the Humanities, Tulane Service Learning, The Schweser Family Foundation, and the guys from the Cultivating Community Program for donating the proceeds from your work with Longue Vue to help us get these books out.

To all of the individuals who have stepped up and given so much—from the donation of stamps to all the folks who have trusted us with their money. To Phyllis Sassoon and Mick Abraham for donating their cars. To all the folks who contributed, from the change jars at Whole Foods to the checks and food donations.

Thanks to our incredible steering committee, GK Darby, Peter Cook, Norbert Estrella, Tim Lupin, and Eliza Wells.

To Kalamu ya Salaam and Jim Randels at SAC, for taking us in and showing us the ropes, and giving us support as we try to grow. If we have done anything right as teachers it is because you have taught us.

To the administration of John McDonogh Senior High, Principal Spencer, and the past principals Winfield and Goodwin, thank you for being such great partners. To Ms. Pratcher and Ms. Tuckerson, thank you and bless you for dealing with all the headaches we cause. And to the staff at John McDonogh, we are so proud to be working with you.

To Elena Reeves and Kenneth Robin at the Tchopshop, thanks for being great designers, and for being such great sports about working with us. And to Jenny LeBlanc and Kyle Bravo at Hot Iron Press, thank you for being great designers/printer and for moving to town.

To Lauren Schug and Heather Booth, for transcribing and transcribing, above and beyond the call of duty.

To Anita Yesho for copy editing at short notice.

To Stephanie Oberhoff, and Communities in Schools- your mission is beautiful and your execution is great.

To Beverly McKenna, thank you for giving us such a beautiful office when we were only a sliver of an idea.

To Gareth Breunlin, who laid out the books and designed the covers. You have made our ideas come out on paper in a way that has honored all of the work and love involved.

To Davey and Jamie for being our dogs.

To Jerry for grant-writing, copy-editing, and being our hero.

To Dan, for his constant input, sharing a car and a computer, writing grants and cooking numerous dinners for the NSP.

To Shana, for promoting this project like it was your own, and for the input and help and grace.

And our biggest thank-you and respect to all of the Bolding, Jackson, Nelson, Price, and Wylie families. Without your love and care, this would not have been possible. Thank you for believing in the project and the work, and for making these books what they are.

And to Palmyra, Lafitte, St. Claude, Dorgenois (and the rest of Ebony's Sixth Ward), and N. Miro, thank you for your stories. We hope you like the books as much we liked making them.

The list is so long because so many of you have contributed.

Thanks for reading.

For the Neighborhood Story Project

Rachel Breunlin
Abram Himelstein

P.S. Thanks to Richard Nash, Ammi Emergency and Soft Skull Press for believing in us and New Orleans in our time of need.